KU-026-738

CityPack
Amsterdam

TERESA FISHER

Teresa Fisher is a freelance journalist who, having lived in mainland Europe for many years, remains a frequent visitor to Holland and, in particular, Amsterdam. She writes regularly for a variety of newspapers, magazines and books at home and abroad, including the recent AA publications Citypack Munich *and* Village France. *When Teresa is not writing she enjoys sailing and skiing.*

City-centre map continues on inside back cover

AA Publishing

Contents

life 5 – 12

how to organise your time 13 – 22

top 25 sights 23 – 48

About this book

KEY TO SYMBOLS

✚	map reference on the fold-out map accompanying this book (see below)	🚌	nearest bus route
✉	address	⛴	nearest riverboat or ferry stop
☎	telephone number	♿	facilities for visitors with disabilities
◔	opening times	✋	admission charge
🍴	restaurant or café on premises or nearby	↔	other nearby places of interest
Ⓜ	nearest underground or Metro train station	❓	tours, lectures, or special events
🚆	nearest overground train station	▶	indicates the page where you will find a fuller description
		ℹ	tourist information

CityPack Amsterdam is divided into six sections to cover the six most important aspects of your visit to Amsterdam. It includes:

- The author's view of the city and its people
- Itineraries, walks and excursions
- The top 25 sights to visit – as selected by the author
- Features about different aspects of the city that make it special
- Detailed listings of restaurants, hotels, shops and nightlife
- Practical information

In addition, easy-to-read side panels provide fascinating extra facts and snippets, highlights of places to visit and invaluable practical advice.

CROSS-REFERENCES

To help you make the most of your visit, cross-references, indicated by ▶, show you where to find additional information about a place or subject.

MAPS

- **The fold-out map** in the wallet at the back of the book is a comprehensive street plan of Amsterdam. All the map references given in the book refer to this map. For example, the Westerkerk in the Westermarkt on Prinsengracht has the following information: ✚ 65 indicating the grid square of the map in which the Westerkerk will be found.
- **The city-centre maps** found on the inside front and back covers of the book itself are for quick reference. They show the Top 25 Sights, described on pages 24–48, which are clearly plotted by number (**1** – **25**, not page number) from west to east.

PRICES

Where appropriate, an indication of the cost of an establishment is given by **£** signs: **£££** denotes higher prices, **££** denotes average prices, while **£** denotes lower charges.

AMSTERDAM
life

A PERSONAL VIEW

Few cities arouse such contradictory feelings in visitors as Amsterdam: old yet modern, beautiful yet sordid, sleepy yet energetic, international in outlook yet provincial in character. One thing on which all agree, though, is that it is the most exciting, sophisticated and alluring of all Dutch cities, and a place which is sure to leave a lasting impression on anyone who goes there.

Strolling along the grand horseshoe-shaped canals of the inner city, with their magnificent patrician mansions, one can easily imagine Amsterdam in its 17th-century heyday, when it became the richest city in Europe, headquarters of an empire and world capital of culture and commerce. Gentlemen's, Emperor's and Prince's Canals: their very names reflect the grandeur of the Golden Age. Over five thousand of the buildings along these canals are classified monuments. At night, fairy lights define the humped-back bridges, and, as the Dutch seldom draw their curtains, you can catch glimpses of their homes at dusk – trendy warehouse conversions, perhaps, or the gilded ceilings of grand salons, all with pot plants the size of half-grown trees and bunches of fresh flowers.

Romantic, picturebook images such as these are easy to find in Amsterdam. Some people wear

In their view

'The town appears to be standing, not on the earth, but on its own reflections' (Karel Capek, 1933).

'Where else in the world are all life's commodities and all conceivable curiosities to be found as easily as here? In what other country can one find such absolute freedom?' (René Descartes, 1631).

'This city seems to be double: one can also see it in the water: and the reflection of these distinguished houses in these canals makes this spot a fairyland' (Jean Francois Regnard, 1681).

The Keizersgracht seen from the tower of the Westerkerk

clogs, cheese is sold in bright yellow rounds, the parks are ablaze with tulips in May, and windmills are on the horizon. Modern Amsterdam is not in the least a quaint, timeless city, though. It has many other aspects, less picturesque perhaps, but more interesting.

One of the defining images of the city is that of the Prostutiezone, or Red Light District, with its sleazy sexshops, the heady scent of dope, and neon-lit, barely clad prostitutes touting for business at their windows. Amsterdam's liberal attitude towards sex still surprises many visitors, but the city has always prided itself on its easygoing attitude. Historically it has been tolerant of minority groups, and over the centuries has provided sanctuary for victims of persecution. As a result, over a hundred different cultures, including many from the former Dutch colonies, now try to live harmoniously in this cosmopolitan city. Its tolerance has also provided the city with problems. Ever since the 1960s, when Amsterdam became the hippie capital of Europe, it has been trying to cope with 'drugs tourism'. Today its 'smoking' coffee shops, where the sale and use of soft drugs is tolerated, are the city's main attraction for many young people from all over Europe.

There is no denying, however, that the atmosphere in Holland's capital has changed over the past 25 years. The hippies, squatters and *provos* (anti-establishment rebels) of the '60s are now the conforming citizens of the '90s. The authorities are trying to play down the old 'capital of counter-culture' image, and to present a more conventional one, of culture and fine arts.

The Netherlands claims the highest concentration of museums in the world, and Amsterdam boasts some of the most famous collections. The Rijksmuseum, with its unrivalled collection of Dutch art and the Rijksmuseum Vincent van

Herring city

If there had been no herring, Amsterdam might never have come into existence. In the Middle Ages, the Dutch discovered a method of curing these fish, and they became a staple food. Herring fishermen built a dam across the river Amstel and a small fishing village developed, called Amstelledamme. Its site is now Dam Square, Amsterdam's main square.

Colourful cheeses are a traditional part of Dutch food

7

Amsterdam in winter has a special charm

Double Dutch

Double Dutch (gibberish), *going Dutch* (sharing expenses equally), *a Dutch treat* (a party or outing for which the participants pay) and *Dutch courage* (false bravery fuelled by alcohol) – the numerous, mostly derogatory 'Dutch' expressions which litter the English language emerged during the 17th century and reflect the British view of their major rivals in maritime trade at the time.

Gogh, are, for many, reason enough to visit the city. The top museums and galleries are clustered near the Concertgebouw, Holland's world-renowned concert hall, favoured by the finest performers of classical music.

Most of the city's cultural and historic sights are packed into a small area. The best way to see them all is on foot or to hurtle around, in true Amsterdam style, on a bicycle. The city is crammed with tiny, quirky shops, offering everything from diamonds to Delftware and from trendy hemp clothing to haute couture. There are bars to suit all moods – dark, cosy 'brown cafés', designer bars and gin-tasting houses (*proeflokalen*). Once businesses close for the day, the outgoing Amsterdammers take to the streets, walking, shopping or drinking in the pavement cafés before eating out at restaurants from around the world, and then moving on to nightspots to tempt even the most jaded visitor. No one could ever describe Amsterdam as dull.

However you *do* choose to describe it – laid-back, paradoxical, impulsive, addictive – this lively, cosmopolitan city masterfully fuses its old-fashioned charm with the furious pace of modern life. Its infinite variety and its ambiguous, unpredictable nature make Amsterdam a city of timeless pleasures. Enjoy!

AMSTERDAM IN FIGURES

- Population (1996): 713,493, including 140 nationalities, 30,000 university students, around 9,000 heroin addicts, 7,000 prostitutes and 3,600 police officers
- Historical growth: 1500 – 9,000 inhabitants; 1550 – 30,000; 1650 – 220,000; 1900 – 510,000; 1963 – 868,000
- 8.5 million tourists visit annually
- Money spent by tourists: f5,000 million

CITY

- Total area of city: 207 sq km
- Area of water: 20 sq km
- Number of districts: 30
- Height: 3m below sea level
- Average temperatures: January 2°C, July 17°C
- Listed buildings: 6,850
- 28 public parks; 220,000 trees; 600,000 flowering bulbs
- Bicycles: 550,000

LEISURE

- 141 art galleries; 60 theatres and concert halls; 42 museums; 40 cinemas; 36 discos
- 1,402 cafés and bars; 755 restaurants; 574 coffee shops
- 10,334 shops

CANALS

- 160 (75km), with 2,400 registered house-boats, 1,281 bridges, 120 waterbikes, 90 islands, and 70 glass-topped *rondvaartboten*
- Cleaned: four times a week
- Rubbish: 100 million litres dredged each year, including up to 10,000 bicycles

On Rembrandtplein, one of Amsterdam's 1,402 cafés

A Chronology

13th century	Herring fishermen settle on the Amstel A dam is built across the Amstel
1300	Amsterdam is given city status
1345	Miracle of Amsterdam (▶ 40) makes the city a pilgrimage centre
1421	The first of several Great Fires
1425	The city's first horseshoe canal is dug, the Singel
1517	Protestant Reformation in Germany. Lutheran and Calvinist ideas take root in Amsterdam
1519	Charles V, King of Spain, crowned Holy Roman Emperor. Amsterdam becomes part of the Spanish empire and nominally Catholic
1566–67	Calvinist iconoclasts riot against Catholicism. The Duke of Alva is sent to restore order, and executes thousands of Protestants
1568	Start of the Dutch Revolt against Spanish rule
1578	The Alteration: Amsterdam capitulates to William of Orange, the Calvinists take power and expel all Catholic leaders from the city
1595–97	First voyage by Dutch traders to Indonesia, via the Cape of Good Hope
17th century	Amsterdam's Golden Age: the city becomes the most important port in the world
1602	Dutch East India Company founded
1613	Work begins on the Grachtengordel (canal ring)
1620	Tulip mania begins
1637	The great tulip crash
1648	End of war with Spain. Dutch Republic is recognised

1652–54	First of numerous wars with England for maritime supremacy
1784	English navy destroys Dutch fleet
1799	Dutch East India Company collapses
1806	Napoleon Bonaparte takes over republic, and establishes his brother Louis Napoleon as king
1813	After defeat of Napoleon, William VI of Orange returns from exile
1876	Opening of the North Sea Canal brings new prosperity to Amsterdam
1880	First use of bicycles in Amsterdam
1914–18	World War I. Netherlands neutral
1928	Amsterdam Olympics
1940	German Occupation
1942	Anne Frank's family go into hiding
1945	Amsterdam liberated by Canadian troops
1940s–50s	Holland withdraws from overseas empire
1952	Opening of the Amsterdam–Rhine Canal
1960s–70s	Hippies from all over Europe flock to the city
1964–67	Series of riots by anti-Establishment 'Provo' (provocateurs) movement
1980	Queen Beatrix crowned
1980	Amsterdam recognised as capital of Holland
1986	Amsterdam celebrates 400th anniversary as a diamond centre
1989	City government falls because of weak anti-vehicle laws. New laws are passed aiming eventually to make Amsterdam free of motor traffic
1990	Van Gogh Centenary exhibition attracts 890,000 visitors

11

PEOPLE & EVENTS FROM HISTORY

A popular monarch

Beatrix, Queen of the Netherlands, came to the throne when her mother, Queen Juliana, abdicated on 30 April 1980. Beatrix was crowned at the Nieuwe Kerk. Her great popularity is reflected in the celebrations on her official birthday (*Koninginnedag* 30 April) – a national holiday, when the entire city becomes one massive, uproarious street party.

WILLIAM OF ORANGE AND THE REVOLT OF THE NETHERLANDS

During the 16th century, the Dutch rebelled against Spain's religious and political oppression. The resistance was led by William I, Prince of Orange, better known as William the Silent. In 1578 he took control of Amsterdam in a bloodless coup called the 'Alteration'. The city's Roman Catholic magistrates and clergy were all deported, and Amsterdam was declared a Calvinist city.

DUTCH EAST INDIA COMPANY (VOC)

In 1602, a number of companies in Amsterdam joined together to create the *Verenigde Oost-Indische Compagnie* (VOC) to control Dutch trading. With bases throughout the Orient, it soon became the world's largest trading company, enjoying tremendous prosperity in the 17th century. Thereafter, due to competition from England and France, it went into decline, and in 1799 was declared bankrupt.

REMBRANDT

Rembrandt Harmenszoon van Rijn (1606–69) was the most creative and influential Dutch artist of the 17th century. Following his marriage to a wealthy heiress in 1634, he spent his most successful years in Amsterdam, as a highly respected painter. However, changing tastes in art, and the untimely death of his wife, Saskia, in 1642, resulted in Rembrandt's impoverishment, though not in any decline in his talent. He eventually died a pauper (➤ 44).

ANNE FRANK

Anne Frank (1929–45) was a Jewish victim of Nazi persecution during World War II. Following two years in hiding from the Gestapo, during which time she kept detailed diaries, her family was arrested and deported to concentration camps. Only her father survived. He published her diaries, which have been translated into more than 55 languages, making Anne Frank the Netherlands' most widely translated author (➤ 31).

AMSTERDAM
how to organise your time

ITINERARIES

These four itineraries take you to some of Amsterdam's main sights. The best way to see the city is on foot or, in true local style, by bicycle. Public transport is easy to use, with efficient bus, tram and metro systems. Almost all places of interest are within walking distance of each other, and the city's layout of concentric canals and criss-crossing streets provides a ready-made orientation grid.

ITINERARY ONE	**HISTORIC CITY**
Morning	Start your tour with a visit to the Amsterdams Historisch Museum (➤35), which will give you an idea of the city's colourful history. Then visit the Begijnhof (➤34), Holland's finest almshouses.
Lunch	Try Caffé Esprit (➤69) or a Dutch speciality restaurant, such as Haesje Claes (➤62).
Afternoon	Enjoy the street entertainment between visits to the sumptuous Koninklijk Paleis (Royal Palace ➤36) and Nieuwe Kerk (➤37), both built on the dam (now Dam Square) which gave Amsterdam its name.
Evening	At dusk, explore the Prostutiezone (Red Light District ➤39), but watch your wallet.
ITINERARY TWO	**ART TREASURES**
Morning	See part of the Rijksmuseum's immense collection (➤28) – start with the paintings of the Golden Age. Then recover in the Vondelpark (➤24).
Lunch	Have lunch in the park or head to Leidseplein (➤27) where there is a wide choice of cafés and restaurants.
Afternoon	Return to the Museumsplein for more art, at the Van Gogh Museum (➤26) or the Stedelijk Museum (➤25), which specialises in modern art – a difficult choice but neither should be missed.

Malevich painting in the Stedelijk Museum

ITINERARY THREE	**MARITIME HISTORY**
Morning	It's easy to imagine 17th-century Amsterdam at its peak of its maritime success, during an early morning stroll around the Western Islands (➤ panel, page 51). A bus ride from here (🚌 **22, 28**) takes you to the Eastern Islands and the Scheepvaart (Maritime) Museum (➤ 47).
Lunch	Enjoy a snack at the Scheepvaart Museum restaurant.
Afternoon	Take bus 22 to the Tropenmuseum (➤ 48) which re-creates tropical scenes, or walk to the Hortus Botanicus (botanical gardens) (➤ 58) beside Artis Zoo (➤ 59). Continue to the Museum Willet-Holthuysen (➤ 42), built for a wealthy merchant of the Golden Age.
Evening	End your day of world travel with a candlelit canal cruise (➤ 19).

Clogs - popular souvenirs though no longer everyday wear

ITINERARY FOUR	**SIGHTSEEING AND SHOPPING**
Morning	Avoid the queues by getting to Anne Frankhuis (➤ 31) early. Then clear your head with an energetic climb up the nearby Westerkerk tower (➤ 30), which has breathtaking views.
Lunch	By now, you will have earned one of the Pancake Bakery's delicious *pannekoeken* (➤ 68).
Afternoon	Explore the Grachtengordel (Canal Ring) (➤ 29, 32, 50–51), and go souvenir shopping in the district's narrow streets (➤ 70–76). Don't forget the Bloemenmarkt (➤ 38) for bulbs and for that special gift, Stoeltie Diamonds (➤ 43).

15

WALKS

*Characteristic gables
along the Singel*

THE SIGHTS

INFORMATION

Distance: 4km
Time: 1–2 hours
Start/Endpoint: Dam
✚ H5
▨ Tram 4, 9, 14, 16, 24, 25

THE CANAL RING AND JORDAAN

After breakfast at La Ruche (► 69) in De Bijenkorf department store, leave Dam Square via Paleisstraat, continue straight on over the scenic Singel, Herengracht and Keizersgracht canals, and then turn right alongside Prinsengracht to pass the impressive tower of the Westerkerk and Anne Frankhuis (Anne Frank's House). Cross over Prinsengracht and double back on yourself for a few yards along the west bank of the canal until you reach the peaceful, leafy Bloemgracht canal. Turn right here, take the second right up Tweede Leliedwarsstraat, cross over Egelantiersgracht, turn right along its shady bank and then immediately left up Tweede Egelantiers Dwarsstraat into the heart of the bohemian Jordaan district. Take time to soak up the atmosphere in one of the numerous cafés and browse awhile in the tiny designer boutiques here.

Walk on to Lijnbaansgracht, and then turn right into Lindengracht, once a canal and now site of a splendid Saturday food market, to reach Brouwersgracht (► 50), one of Amsterdam's most attractive canals, lined with traditional Dutch barges and houseboats. Pause for a pre-lunch drink at the Papeneiland 'brown café' (reputedly Amsterdam's oldest café ► 80) on the corner of Prinsengracht. Cross Brouwersgracht at Herengracht and continue along Brouwersgracht to the Singel. Cross by the sluice gates and turn right along the eastern side of the Singel, past Amsterdam's smallest house (No. 7) and the Poezenboot – a houseboat refuge for stray cats. To conclude the walk, turn left at Torenstraat, cross Spui and go along Molensteeg. Continue across Nieuwezijds Voorburgwal, past Nieuwe Kerk on the left and return to Dam Square, for a tasty lunch of Dutch specialities at De Roode Leeuw (► 62).

MARKETS AND MUSEUMS

Leaving Dam Square via Paleisstraat, turn left onto Nieuwezijds Voorburgwal, where a stamp and coin market is held (the Postzegelmarkt ➤ 53). About 100 metres further on the left, narrow Sint Luciensteeg leads to the Amsterdams Historisch Museum. Pass through the Schuttersgalerij (Civic Guard Gallery) into a narrow lane of whitewashed houses called Gedempte Begijnsloot. At the southern end, a stone archway on your right brings you into the calm of the leafy, cobbled, Begijnhof courtyard. A further archway leads to Spui which, with its cluster of pavement cafés, makes a good coffee stop on a sunny day. On Fridays, you will find a bustling market of antiquarian books here, and on Sundays the stalls sell paintings and prints.

Head southwest from Spui and turn left along the edge of the Singel. Cross the bridge into Koningsplein and Amsterdam's ravishing flower market, the Bloemenmarkt, a photographer's paradise. Your next landmark, the Munttoren (Mint Tower) at Muntplein, is easy to spot. Turn right along the Amstel and follow it just past the Blauwbrug (Blue Bridge). Turn right along Herengracht to make a short detour to the Willet-Holthuysen Museum, which gives a rare glimpse inside one of the canal's elegant patrician mansions. On your return, cross the bridge to reach the Waterlooplein fleamarket, a hotch-potch of stalls, some with trendy clothes and others cluttered with junk. Tucked away at the far end of the market is the Museum het Rembrandthuis (Rembrandt's House), a sight not to be missed. End your walk with a drink on the terrace of Café Dantzig (➤ 68) opposite the Muziek Theater or Stopera (➤ 55), and watch the barges chugging up the Amstel River.

THE SIGHTS

- Amsterdams Historisch Museum (➤ 35)
- Begijnhof (➤ 34)
- Markets (➤ 53)
- Singel (➤ 33)
- Bloemenmarkt (➤ 38)
- Munttoren (➤ 55)
- Blauwbrug (➤ 54)
- Museum Willet-Holthuysen (➤ 42)
- Museum het Rembrandthuis (➤ 44)

INFORMATION

Distance: 2.5km
Time: 1–2 hours
Startpoint: Dam Square
➕ H5
🚊 Tram 4, 9, 14, 16, 24, 25
Endpoint: Café Dantzig
➕ H5
Ⓜ Waterlooplein

Waterlooplein fleamarket

EVENING STROLLS

*Red Light District signs
pull no punches*

PROSTUTIEZONE
(RED LIGHT DISTRICT)

From Dam Square, turn up Warmoesstraat (by Hotel Krasnapolsky), the city's oldest street. After the police station, turn right down Lange Niezel and then right again at Oudezijds Voorburgwal, past the Oude Kerk (► 40), incongruous in this seedy place. Cross the canal at Stoofstraat, then turn right on to Oudezijds Achterburgwal, pass the Hash Marijuana Hemp Museum, cross the bridge and follow Oude Hoogstraat to the 'pill-bridge' (Pillenbrug), often crowded with junkies by the drug-paraphernalia hangout, the Head Shop. Cross the bridge and go left (north) up Kloevenierburgswal to the Waag (the old weigh-house) at Nieuwmarkt. Turn left back to Oudezijds Achterburgwal, then right along the canal past the Tattoo Museum and the Erotic Museum. At the canal's end, go right along Vredenburgerstraat to Zeedijk (► 52). Follow the road to the left round to Warmoesstraat for dinner. Return to Dam Square.

SQUARES AND CANALS

Head south across Thorbeckeplein from the neon lights and pulsating cafés of Rembrandtplein, and turn left on to the silent, stately Herengracht (► 32). Turn right onto the Amstel for a view of the illuminated Skinny Bridge (► 45). The next right takes you back along Keizersgracht to the enchanting Reguliersgracht. Turn right and then left to reach Herengracht's magically lit 'Golden Bend'. Cross over Vijzelstraat, then turn left and follow Nieuwe Spiegelstraat, passing countless antique shops, as far as Lijnbaansgracht. Turn right here and at the canal's end cut across Max Euweplein, past the glitzy Casino and along the Lido, to reach the lively Leidseplein (► 27).

SAFETY

Amsterdam has a high rate of pickpocketing and muggings. The main problem areas are the markets and museums, Centraal Station, Schiphol Airport and the Red Light District. At night, keep to well-lit, well-populated areas.

ORGANISED SIGHTSEEING

ON THE WATER

Holland International ✉ Prins Hendrikkade 33a
☎ 6227788 🕐 Apr-Oct A large company, offering
cruises every 15 minutes
in glass-topped boats,
called *rondvaartboten*.
Canal Bus Tours ✉ Wete-
ingschans 24 ☎ 6239886 A water-
bus service goes around the
city, and there are also two
theme tours: *Rembrandt* and
City on the Water.
Rederijk Lovers Amsterdam
✉ Prins Hendrikkade 25–27
☎ 6222181 🕐 Daily in summer, fewer
in winter Canal cruises for
romantics, with candlelight
and soft music as well
as a commentary, and
refreshments.
Museumboat ✉ Stationsplein 8
☎ 6222181 A service every
half-hour, linking seven
jetties near the 20 major
museums, enables you to
combine canal cruising
with museum visits. A day ticket costs f22.

*A boat tour gives a
different view*

ON DRY LAND

Yellow Bike Tours ✉ Nieuwezijds Kolk 29 ☎ 6206940
☎ Daily Apr-Oct See the city at a sedate pace or
head out to the spectacular waterlands north of
Amsterdam to visit windmills and a clog
factory.
Tourist Tram ✉ Centraal Station ☎ 5514911 Sun, in summer &
holidays An hourly tram service around the city
sights.
Amsterdam Travel and Tours ✉ Dam 10 ☎ 6276236
🕐 Mar to mid-Nov Organised walking tours include
Hidden Areas, The Jordaan and, by night, *The Red
Light District.*

FROM THE AIR

KLM Helicopter Tours ✉ Schiphol Airport ☎ 747747
🕐 Depends on weather Breathtaking aerial views of
Amsterdam and its environs.

Watery ways

Seeing Amsterdam from the water
is an unforgettable experience.
Alternatives to the glass-topped
tourboats are a water taxi
(✉ Stationsplein 8
☎ 6222181), or a pedal boat
rented from Canal Bike
(✉ Weteringschans 24
☎ 6265574) for f12.50 an hour
(with a deposit of f50).
Remember that boat traffic keeps
to the right-hand side of the
waterways.

EXCURSIONS

INFORMATION

Haarlem
Distance: 20km west
Journey time: 17 min
- Train from
  Centraal Station
- Stationsplein 1
- 06/32034043

Keukenhof
Distance: 39km southwest
Journey time: 1 hour
- Combined rail/bus/admission
  tickets from Centraal Station
- Lisse
- 02521/19034
- End Mar–end May daily 8–6
- Very expensive

Delft
Distance: 50km southwest
Journey time: 30 min
- Train from Centraal Station to
  The Hague then change for
  Delft
- Markt 85
- 015/2126100

Edam
Distance: 15km north
Journey time: 20 min
- Bus from Centraal Station
- Damplein 1
- 02993/71727

HAARLEM

As you wander through the historic heart of Haarlem it is hard to believe that this is the eighth largest city in Holland and the centre of Dutch printing, pharmaceutical and bulb-growing industries. The brick-paved, traffic-free streets are lined with elegant Renaissance buildings, and have hardly changed since the town's 17th-century heyday. For centuries, the town's main meeting place has been the lively main square – Grote Markt – today bordered with busy pavement cafés. Nearby, the Grote Kerk boasts one of the world's largest and finest organs, an ornate instrument which has drawn many renowned composers to the city, including Handel and Mozart. Haarlem's greatest attraction, however, is the Frans Hals Museum, home of the best collection of works by this painter. A short cruise can be taken along the river from the Gravenstenenbrug lift bridge.

KEUKENHOF BULB GARDENS

Located at the heart of the *Bloembollenstreek*, the bulb-growing region (literally 'bulb-stretch'), Keukenhof ranks among the most famous gardens of the world. The site – 28 ha of wooded park on the outskirts of Lisse – was acquired in 1949 as a showcase. Try to visit between March and late May, when over seven million bulbs are in bloom, laid out in brilliant swathes of red, yellow, pink and blue. Few people leave without a bag of bulbs for their own gardens.

Keukenhof Gardens blaze with colour

DELFT

The name of Delft is known the world over for its blue-and-white pottery (see panel), and this charming old town was also the birthplace of the artist Johannes Vermeer (1632–75). His simple grave can be seen in the Oude Kerk along with those of other eminent Delft citizens, including Antonie van Leeuwenhoek, inventor of the microscope.

William of Orange (➤ 12) led his revolt against Spanish rule from the Prinsenhof in Delft. The building now houses the city museum, which includes a collection of rare antique Delftware. You can still see the bullet holes halfway up the stairs where William was murdered in 1584. His elaborate marble tomb, designed by Hendrick de Keyser in 1614, lies in the Nieuwe Kerk.

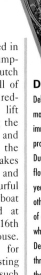

EDAM

Famous for its ball-shaped cheeses wrapped in wax (red for export, yellow for local consumption), Edam is everyone's idea of a typical Dutch town – exceptionally picturesque and full of narrow tree-shaded canals lined by gabled, red-roofed houses and crossed by wooden lift bridges. Edam enjoyed its heyday during the Golden Age when shipbuilding, fishing and cheese brought economic prosperity to the town. A traditional cheese market still takes place on Wednesday mornings in July and August. The colourful cheeses arrive by boat and are weighed at the Kaasmarkt's 16th century weigh-house. The method for producing long-lasting pressed cheeses such as Edam and Gouda was perfected in the Middle Ages, and is much the same today, though now the process is automated.

Delftware

Delftware was developed from majolica in the 16th century, by immigrant Italian potters who produced wall tiles with motifs of Dutch landscapes, animals and flowers. Over the next hundred years, trade with the east brought other influences, particularly that of delicate Chinese porcelain which led to finer work. By 1652 De Porceleyne Fles was one of 32 thriving potteries here. Today it is the only original Delftware factory in production, and offers daily guided tours.

What's On

Amsterdam's year is punctuated with numerous fairs, festivals and street parties celebrating eveything from cycling to Santa Claus, including the party to end all parties, the Queen's birthday.

Pick up a copy of the main English-language listings magazine *What's On*, available from newsagents and tourist offices, or the free monthly *Amsterdam Times*, obtainable from big hotels. *Uitkrant*, in Dutch, is accessible to non-Dutch speakers and contains comprehensive details of cultural events.

FEBRUARY	Carnival, celebrated as a preamble to Lent. Dockers' Strike Commemoration (25 Feb ➤ 46)
MARCH	Stille Omgang (second Sun): silent procession celebrating Amsterdam's miracle (➤ 40)
APRIL	National Museum Weekend (mid-month): Free or reduced entrance to all museums. Koninginnedag (30 Apr): the Queen's birthday World Press Photos (end-Apr): Exhibition
MAY	Remembrance Day (4 May): Two minutes silence at 8pm following a ceremony at Dam Square in remembrance of World War II victims. Liberation Day (5 May): Street parties, speeches and concerts celebrate the end of the German occupation in 1945. National Windmill Day (second Sat, ➤ 60) National Cycling Day (second Sun)
JUNE	Holland Festival: International arts festival. Open-air Theatre Season (until mid-August): in Vondelpark (➤ 24). Grachtenloop canal race (second Sun): along the banks of Prinsengracht and Vijzelgracht
JULY	Summer Festival: alternative arts festival
AUGUST	Dammen Op De Dam (mid-Aug): open-air draughts tournament in Dam Square. Prinsengracht concert (last Fri): classical music recitals on canal barges
SEPTEMBER	Bloemencorso (first Sat): parade of flower-laden floats from Aalsmeer to Amsterdam. National Monument Day (second Sat): monuments and buildings, usually closed, are open. Jordaan Folk Festival (middle weeks)
OCTOBER	Antiques Fair
NOVEMBER	Sinterklaas Parade (➤ 57)
DECEMBER	*Pakjesavond* (5 Dec): parcel evening, Holland's traditional day for present giving (➤ 57). *Oudejaarsavond* (31 Dec): New Years' Eve – wild street parties, fireworks, and popping champagne corks herald the new year

AMSTERDAM's
top 25 sights

The sights are shown on the maps on the inside front cover and inside back cover, numbered **1–25** from west to east across the city

1

VONDELPARK

DID YOU KNOW?

- The sumptuous Art Deco interior of the Dutch Film Museum was rescued from Amsterdam's first cinema, the Cinema Parisien
- Over 1,000 new and classic films are shown every year

INFORMATION

- ✚ E7–G6
- ✉ Stadhouderskade
- ◎ Dawn–dusk daily
- 🍴 Café Vertigo (££), Het Ronde Blauwe Theehouse (££)
- 🚋 Tram 1, 2, 3, 5, 6, 12
- 🚢 Museumboat stop 2
- ♿ Good
- ↔ Stedelijk Museum (➤ 25), Van Gogh Museum (➤ 26), Leidseplein (➤ 27)
- ❓ Open-air summer festival of theatre and concerts

Open-air auditorium in Vondelpark

"One of my favourite places for people-watching. Among the joggers, sunbathers, frisbee-throwers and bookworms, let yourself be entertained by the musicians, mime artists and acrobats in this welcome splash of green near the city centre."

Pleasure gardens Amsterdam's largest and oldest municipal park – a vast 48ha rectangle of former marshland – was first opened in 1865. The designers, J D and L P Zocher, intentionally moved away from the symmetrical Dutch garden, creating a romantic English-style garden with lengthy sweeps of pathway, open lawns, ornamental lakes, meadows and woodland. Financed by wealthy local residents, the Nieuwe Park became the heart of a new luxurious residential district. Two years later, a statue of Holland's best-known playwright, Joost van den Vondel (1587–1679) – the Shakespeare of the Netherlands – was erected in the park and its present name was adopted. Today, thanks to its wide open spaces, children's playgrounds, bandstand, tea-houses and fragrant rose-garden, it remains one of the city's most popular choices for family outings. It is also the venue of the Dutch Film Museum, an absolute must for cinephiles.

Hippie mecca The Vondelpark has always been a colourful place, but its heyday was in the 1970s when hippies flocked to Amsterdam, attracted by the city's tolerant attitude to soft drugs. Vondelpark soon became their main gathering point, with thousands camping in the open and creating a summer-long pop festival atmosphere, until the end of the decade when the bubble burst and the hippies were forced to disperse. All that remains are buskers, flea markets and the occasional ageing hippy.

STEDELIJK MUSEUM

"Undoubtedly one of the world's leading museums of modern art. From Matisse to Malevich and Mondrian, from Klee to Kandinsky and Keinholz, this gallery is an absolute must for art enthusiasts."

Controversial collection The Stedlijk or City Museum, Amsterdam's foremost venue for contemporary art, was founded in 1895. Its collection of over 25,000 paintings, sculptures, drawings, graphics and photos contains some of the great names of modern art (Van Gogh, Cézanne, Picasso, Monet, Chagall) but the main emphasis is on progressive post-war movements and the very latest, often highly controversial, trends in contemporary art. There is not enough space to keep the entire collection on permanent display but an extension is planned for the 21st century.

House of Museums In 1938 the Stedelijk became Holland's National Museum of Modern Art, but it achieved its worldwide avant-garde reputation in 1945–63, when it was under the dynamic direction of Willem Sandberg. He abandoned the old collections and created a House of Museums in which art, photography, dance, theatre, music and cinema were all represented, through innovative and sometimes shocking exhibitions.

Cutting edge of art Museum highlights include suprematist paintings by Malevich; works by Mondrian, Rietveld and other exponents of the Dutch *De Stijl* school; and a remarkable collection of almost childlike paintings by the *CoBrA* movement, founded in defiance of the artistic complacency of post-war Europe, and named after the native cities of its members – Copenhagen, Brussels and Amsterdam.

HIGHLIGHTS

- The Parakeet and the Mermaid (Matisse, 1952–3)
- The Women of the Revolution (Kiefer, 1986)
- My Name as Though it were Written on the Surface of the Moon (Nauman, 1986)
- Sitting Woman with Fish Hat (Picasso, 1942)
- The Appelbar (Appel, 1951)
- Beanery (Kienholz, 1965)
- Rietveld furniture collection

INFORMATION

- ✚ G6
- ✉ Paulus Potterstraat 13
- ☎ 5732911
- ◷ Daily 11–5, public holidays 11–4. Closed 1 Jan
- 🍴 Restaurant (££)
- 🚃 Tram 2, 3, 5, 12, 16
- ♿ Very good
- 🎟 Moderate
- ↔ Vondelpark (➤ 24), Rijksmuseum Vincent van Gogh (➤ 26), Rijksmuseum (➤ 28)
- ❓ Lectures, films and concerts. Book guided tours

Top: Special exhibitions are a feature of the Stedelijk Museum

3

RIJKSMUSEUM VINCENT VAN GOGH

HIGHLIGHTS

- The Potato Eaters, 1885
- Self-portrait as a Painter, 1888
- Bedroom at Arles, 1888
- Vase with Sunflowers, 1888
- Wheatfield with Crows, 1890

DID YOU KNOW?

- Van Gogh sold only one painting in his life
- Record price for a van Gogh painting is f93million (1990 Portrait of Dr Gachet)

INFORMATION

- ✚ G6
- ✉ Paulus Potterstraat 7
- ☎ 5705200
- ◷ Daily 10–5. Closed 1 Jan
- 🍴 Self-service restaurant (££)
- 🚋 Tram 2,5
- 🚤 Museumboat stop 3
- ♿ Excellent
- 💷 Expensive
- ↔ Stedelijk Museum (► 25)
  Rijksmuseum (► 28)

Top: Bedroom at Arles.
Below: self portrait

" Even if you are not an art–lover, it is undeniably a moving experience to trace this great artist's tragic life and extraordinary achievements, through such a comprehensive display of masterworks. "

World's largest van Gogh collection Of his 900 paintings and 1,200 drawings, the Van Gogh Museum boasts 200 and 500 respectively. They were donated by his younger brother, Theo, together with 850 letters, his Japanese print collection, and works by friends and influential contemporaries, including Gauguin, Monet, Bernard and Pissarro. Van Gogh's paintings are arranged chronologically, starting with works from 1880–87, a period characterised by realistic landscape paintings and peasant scenes in dark, heavy tones, in the tradition of Old Masters. This period is typified by *The Potato Eaters* of 1885.

Colourful palette The broad brush strokes and bold colours that characterise van Gogh's works of 1887–90 reflect the influence of his move to Paris in 1886 and the effect of Impressionism seen in his street and café scenes. Tired of city life, he moved in 1888 to Arles where, intoxicated by the intense sunlight and the brilliant colours of Provence, he painted many of his finest works. He loved the sun, and yellow became increasingly predominant in his paintings, including *Harvest at La Crau* and the *Sunflowers* series.

Final years After snipping off a bit of his ear and offering it to a local prostitute, van Gogh voluntarily entered an asylum in St Remy, where his art took an expressionistic form. His mental anguish may be seen in the way he painted gnarled trees and menacing skies, as in the desolate *Wheatfield with Crows*. Shortly after completing this picture, he shot himself, aged 37.

LEIDSEPLEIN

" *For me this square represents Amsterdam's nightlife at its vibrant best. It is filled with overflowing pavement cafés, ablaze with neon lights and abuzz with jugglers, buskers and fire-eaters. Make sure you spend at least one evening here.* **"**

Party atmosphere Leidseplein has been a centre of activity for centuries. During the Middle Ages, farmers on their way to market unloaded their carts here, at the outskirts of the city. At the turn of the century, artists and writers gathered here; in the 1930s Leidseplein was the site of many clashes between political factions, and it became the main site for anti-Nazi rallies during the war. In the 1960s it was the stamping ground of the *Pleiners* (Dutch Mods), and in 1992 it was the venue for wild celebrations following Ajax's UEFA Cup victory. Today, despite the constant flow of trams through the square, it is always alive with fire-eaters, sword-swallowers and other street entertainment. By night, the dazzling neon lights and crowded café terraces seating over 1,000 people transform the square into one of Amsterdam's liveliest nightlife centres, pulsating until the early hours. Look out for two notable buildings both classified as protected monuments: the distinctive red-brick Stadsschouwburg (Municipal Theatre), with its wide verandah and little turrets, and the art nouveau American Hotel, with its striking art deco café.

Winter wonderland Whatever the season Leidseplein remains one of the city's main meeting places. In winter, when most tourists have returned home, it becomes quintessentially Dutch. A skating rink becomes the centre of attention as locals huddle together for a drink and a chat. It is also *the* place to be on New Year's Eve.

HIGHLIGHTS

- American Hotel (1904)
- Stadsschouwburg (1894)
- Street entertainment
- Winter ice-rink

INFORMATION

- ✚ G6
- ✉ Leidseplein
- 🍴 Restaurants and cafés (£–£££)
- 🚊 Tram 1, 2, 5, 6, 7, 10
- 🚌 Museumboat stop 2
- ↔ Vondelpark (➤ 24), Rijksmuseum (➤ 28), Prinsengracht (➤ 29)

Top: cafés in Leidseplein at night. Below: a stilt walker entertains

5

RIJKSMUSEUM

INFORMATION

- ➕ G6
- ✉ Stadhouderskade 42
- ☎ 6732121
- ◷ Daily 10–5. Closed 1 Jan
- 🍴 Café/restaurant (££)
- 🚃 Tram 2, 5, 6, 7, 10
- 🚤 Museumboat stop 3
- ♿ Very good
- 💶 Expensive
- ↔ Stedelijk Museum (➤ 25), Rijksmuseum Vincent van Gogh (➤ 26)
- ❓ Audio-tour

Top: The Merry Family, Jan Steen. *Below:* Self-portrait as the Apostle Paul, *Rembrandt*

" *Allow plenty of time to visit the Rijksmuseum, and visit more than once if you can. This is Holland's largest museum, with an overwhelming seven million works of art, including the best collection of Dutch art in the world.* **"**

Masterpieces Housed in a palatial red-brick building designed by P J H Cuypers and opened in 1885, the Rijksmuseum boasts an unrivalled collection of Old Master paintings in over 250 rooms, a library with 250,000 volumes, a million prints and drawings, and thousands of sculptures and other artefacts. The first floor of the museum traces the course of Dutch painting from religious works of the medieval era to the rich paintings of the Renaissance and the Golden Age, including works by Rembrandt, Vermeer, Hals and Steen. Pride of place goes to Rembrandt's *The Night Watch* of 1642. This vast, dramatic canvas – one of his largest and most famous compositions, portraying a militia company – is a showpiece of Dutch 17th-century art. It was originally even bigger, but Rembrandt cut it down quite considerably, reputedly to get it through a doorway. In the previous room, a copy of *The Night Watch* attributed to Lundens shows it in its original form.

Treasures Along with the remarkable Dutch paintings other riches in the museum include a collection of Delftware and Meissen porcelain, countless sculptures and Asiatic treasures, a fascinating section on Dutch history, and two ingeniously made doll's houses – scaled-down copies of old canal houses with sumptuous furnishings in keeping. The refurbished south wing of the museum contains a magnificent collection of Dutch Romantic and Amsterdam Impressionist paintings.

PRINSENGRACHT

"Of the three canals that make up the Grachtengordel (Canal Ring), for me Prinsengracht is in many ways the most atmospheric. I love its blend of magnificent merchants' homes, converted old warehouses and tatty, flower-laden houseboats."

Prince William's canal Prinsengracht ('Prince's Canal'), named after William of Orange (▶ 12), was dug at the same time as Herengracht and Keizersgracht, as part of a massive 17th-century expansion scheme. Together these three form the city's distinctive horseshoe-shaped canal network. Less exclusive than the other two waterways, with smaller houses, Prinsengracht became an important thorough-fare of warehouses and merchant's homes. Cargo would be unloaded from ships into fourth-storey storehouses by means of the massive hoist-beams seen today in the gables of many buildings (and still used for lifting furniture). Some houses were built with a deliberate tilt, to protect their façades from the goods as they were hoisted.

Floating homes Some of Amsterdam's most beautiful houseboats are moored along Prinsengracht, near Brouwersgracht or along-side the ivy-covered quays close to the Amstel. Amsterdammers have long lived in houseboats, but a big increase took place during the hous-ing crisis after World War II. Officially there are over 2,400 houseboats in Amsterdam, all with a postal address and mains electricity. The unofficial figure is a lot higher. You will see a variety of craft on Prinsengracht, some more seaworthy than others, ranging from solid old Rhine barges to chalet-like rafts, boats with greenhouses and gardens, and trendy studio homes.

HIGHLIGHTS

- Amstelkerk (▶ 57)
- Anne Frankhuis (▶ 31)
- Noorderkerk (▶ 57)
- Noordermarkt (▶ 53)
- Westerkerk (▶ 30)

DID YOU KNOW?

- Prinsengracht is 4.5km long, 2m deep and 25m wide to accommodate 4 lanes of shipping.
- A law (dating from 1565) restricts the lean of canal houses to 1:25.

INFORMATION

- ✚ G4–6, H6
- 🍴 Bars, cafés, restaurants (£–£££)
- 🚊 Tram 1, 2, 4, 5, 13, 14, 16, 17, 24, 25
- 🚤 Museumboat stop 1
- 🔁 Herengracht (▶ 32), Anne Frankhuis (▶ 31), Westerkerk (▶ 30)

7

WESTERKERK

HIGHLIGHTS

- Climbing the tower
- Organ (Johannes Duyschot 1686)
- Anne Frank statue (Mari Andriessen)
- Rembrandt memorial column
- Grave of Rembrandt's son, Titus

DID YOU KNOW?

- The church was consecrated in 1631
- The tower contains 48 bells
- The largest bell weighs 7,500kg and its hammer weight is 200kg.

INFORMATION

- ✛ G5
- ✉ Prinsengracht 281, Westermarkt
- ☎ 6247766
- 🕐 Sun services only. Tower: Apr–Sep, Mon–Sat 10–4
- 🚊 Tram 13, 14, 17
- 🚤 Museumboot stop 1
- ♿ None
- 🎫 Cheap (tower)
- ↔ Prinsengracht (➤ 29), Anne Frankhuis (➤ 31)
- ❓ Carillon concerts most Tue at noon

"*In my opinion, this is the most beautiful of the four churches built in the 17th century to the north, south, east and west of the city centre. The views from the tower are unsurpassable.***"**

Masterwork The West Church boasts the largest nave of any Dutch Protestant church, the tallest tower and the largest congregation in Amsterdam, and is the church most visited by tourists in the city. It is considered to be the masterwork of Dutch architect Hendrick de Keyser, who died in 1621, one year after building began. Designed to serve the wealthy bourgeoisie living in the smart new mansions of the Canal Ring, it was eventually completed by his son Pieter and Cornelis Dancker in 1631. They added to its tower the gaudy golden crown – a constantly recurring symbol of the city, granted to the citizens by Emperor Maximilian of Austria 150 years earlier. The sweeping views over the gables of Prinsengracht from the top of the tower, popularly called 'Langer Jan' (Tall John), justify the 85m climb. Outside the church, people often lay wreaths at the foot of the statue of Anne Frank (➤ 31), who used to listen to the church bells while she was in hiding, before they were melted down by the Nazis.

Interior The simple, whitewashed interior is laid out in the shape of a double Greek cross. The massive organ is decorated with musical instruments and frescoes of the Evangelists by Gerard de Lairesse, one of Rembrandt's pupils. Rembrandt himself was buried here on 8 October 1669; although no trace of his pauper's grave remains, there is a memorial to him in the north aisle, near the grave of his son, Titus. The church is open only for Sunday services, but you can climb the tower during the week.

ANNE FRANKHUIS

"My greatest wish is to be a journalist, and later on, a famous writer...after the war, I'd like to publish a book called 'The Secret Annexe'. It remains to be seen whether I'll succeed, but my diary can serve as a basis."

Unfulfilled wish On Thursday 11 May 1944, just under three months before she was captured by the Nazis, Anne Frank wrote these poignant words in her Diary. She never saw it published, but died in the concentration camp at Belsen near the end of World War II, aged 15.

'The Secret Annexe' After Nazi Germany invaded the Netherlands in 1940, increasingly severe anti-Semitic measures were introduced. In 1942, the Frank and van Daan families went into hiding here. For the next two years, Anne Frank kept a diary describing daily life – the isolation and the fear of discovery – until the families' betrayal to the Nazis in 1944. Her father was the only member of the group to survive. In 1947, following her wishes, he published her Diary, calling it *Het Achterhuis* (The Secret Annexe). Today, the Annexe attracts over half a million visitors annually, through the entrance concealed by a revolving bookcase, into the small, gloomy rooms so vividly described in the Diary. The building is preserved by the Anne Frank Foundation, an organisation founded to combat racism and anti-Semitism and to promote 'the ideals set down in the Diary of Anne Frank'. In one entry Anne wrote 'I want to go on living even after my death!' As her Diary continues to be read around the world, this wish is fulfilled, and it is sure to go on touching the hearts and minds of generations to come.

DID YOU KNOW?

- The Nazis occupied Amsterdam for five years
- Only 16,000 of the city's 140,000 Jews survived

INFORMATION

- ✚ G4
- ✉ Prinsengracht 263
- ☎ 5567100
- 🕐 Mon–Sat 9–5, Sun and hols 10–5; Jun–Sep daily 9–7. Closed 25 Dec, 1 Jan, Yom Kippur
- 🚊 Tram 13, 14, 17
- 🚤 Museumboat stop 1
- ♿ None
- 💷 Expensive
- ↔ Prinsengracht (▶ 29), Westerkerk (▶ 30)
- ❓ 5-minute introductory film.

Top: the revolving bookcase. Below: sculpture of Anne Frank

HERENGRACHT

"Exploring the city's grandest canal is like going back through time to Amsterdam's Golden Age. These gilded houses are a rich mosaic of Dutch architectural styles spanning four centuries."

The Gentlemen's Canal Herengracht takes its name from the rich merchants and traders of Amsterdam's heyday and is one of three concentric canals built to provide housing for the city's fast-growing population early in the 17th century. The first to be built, it attracted the wealthiest merchant aristocrats and has the largest, most ostentatious houses, 400 of which are now protected monuments. The houses had to conform to many building standards. Even the colour of the front doors – 'Amsterdam green' – was regulated. Taxes were levied according to the width of the canal frontage, hence the rows of tall, narrow residences.

Gable-spotting Canal house-owners stamped their own individuality on properties by means of heavily decorated gables and façades, and you can find every imaginable design along Herengracht. The earliest and most common are the *step* gable and the *spout* gable. Amsterdam's first *neck* gable (No 168) was built in 1638 by Philip Vingboons, and the *bell* gable became popular early in the 18th century. Around this time, Louis XIV-style façades were fashionable. Number 475 is a fine example – nicknamed 'the jewel of canal houses'.

The Golden Bend Amsterdam's most extravagant mansions, with double fronts, were built between Leidsestraat and Vijzelstraat, along the stretch of the canal since dubbed the 'Golden Bend'. To this day, it remains the most prestigious address in town.

Top: a bell gable beside the Herengracht

SINGEL

"You would be forgiven for initially thinking that this canal looks like any other major waterway in the city. Look a little closer though and you will discover some of Amsterdam's most unusual and enchanting sights."

Former city 'belt' From its construction in the early 15th century until the late 16th century, the Singel (originally spelt *Cingle*, meaning 'belt') marked the city limits and was the city's defensive moat. Then, in 1586, the city council decided to build quays along the Singel's west bank and to convert the moat into a canal for large freight ships. Thus the Singel became the first of Amsterdam's concentric canals, and its curved shape established the horseshoe layout of the city. With the coming of the railways, canal transportation became less important and the Singel began to acquire a more residential character. Today, many warehouses have been converted into canalside homes.

Flowers and floating felines Perhaps the most unusual house is at No 7. Its façade is no wider than a front door, making it the narrowest house in Amsterdam. It was built in this way because, during the 17th century, taxes were levied on property according to the width of the frontage. Opposite is the *Poezenboot* - a houseboat for stray cats. Look out too for the 'anti-war' barge further upstream, and the 17th-century prison cell incorporated in the Torensluis (Tower Lock, the Singel's widest bridge) and barely above water level. The beautiful Bloemenmarkt, Europe's only floating flower market, is also on the Singel.

HIGHLIGHTS

- Anti-war barge
- Poezenboot
- Bloemenmarkt (► 38)
- Torensluis prison cell
- Munttoren (► 55)
- No 7: narrowest house
- Nos 2, 36, 74, 83: unusual façades

INFORMATION

- ⊞ H4, G5–H5
- ✉ Singel
- 🕐 Poezenboot: 1–4PM daily
- 🍴 Cafés and restaurants (£–£££)
- 🚊 Tram 13, 14, 17
- ♿ Poezenboot: none
- 💰 Poezenboot: free
- ↔ Bloemenmarkt (► 38), Herengracht (► 32), Koninklijk Paleis (► 36), Begijnhof (► 34)

The Bloemenmarkt brings a riot of colour to the Singel

BEGIJNHOF

DID YOU KNOW?

- The last Begijn died in 1971
- The Pilgrim Fathers are said to have worshipped here before crossing the Atlantic in the *Mayflower*

INFORMATION

- ✚ H5
- ✉ Gedempte Begijnsloot (entrance in Spui)
- ◷ Dawn till dusk
- 🚋 Tram 1, 2, 5
- ♿ Good
- 💲 Free
- ↔ Amsterdams Historisch Museum (➤ 35), Singel (➤ 33)

Below: one of Amsterdam's oldest buildings, the Wooden House

*"A hallowed atmosphere characterises Amsterdam's many **hofjes** (almshouses) but none is more venerable than this leafy oasis of tranquillity. The cobbled courtyard, edged with delightful buildings resembling doll's houses, looks almost like a film set."*

Pious women A tiny, unlikely-looking gateway leads to the Begijnhof, the oldest and finest *hofje* in the country. This secluded community of magnificently restored old houses and gardens clustered around a small church lies a stone's throw from the main shopping thoroughfare. It was built in 1346 as a sanctuary for the *Begijntjes* or Beguines, a religious order of unmarried women who wanted to live in a religious community without becoming nuns. In return for modest lodging, they devoted themselves to the care of the poor and sick. Today, the Begijnhof is a residence for single women earning less than f35,000 a year, and has a five-year waiting list.

Two churches The Begijnkerk (1419), which dominates the courtyard, was confiscated from the Beguines when Amsterdam became Protestant in the Alteration of 1578 (➤ 12). The women continued to worship secretly in one of the houses, until religious tolerance was restored, over 200 years later, in 1795. Their precious church became a warehouse until 1607, when it was given to the Presbyterian community and renamed the Engelse Kerk (English Church). The simple interior contains pulpit panels designed by Piet Mondrian. Nearby, Het Houten Huys (the Wooden House 1477) is one of only two remaining wooden-fronted houses in Amsterdam. It was built prior to the law of 1521, preventing the use of wood as a building material, following a series of fires.

AMSTERDAMS HISTORISCH MUSEUM

"Do make this excellent museum your first port of call. Once you have a grasp of Amsterdam's colourful history you will find subsequent walks around town all the more rewarding."

The building This fun, informative museum traces the growth of Amsterdam from 13th-century fishing village to bustling metropolis, through an impressive collection of paintings, maps, models and historical artefacts. They are displayed chronologically in one of the city's oldest buildings. Originally a monastery, it was occupied for nearly 400 years by the city orphanage (Burgerweeshuis), until 1975 when it was converted into a museum. Most of the present structure dates from the 16th and 17th centuries. Throughout, you can still find evidence of its former use, such as the ceiling paintings in the Regent's Chamber, and the numerous portraits of children, such as Jan Carel van Speyck who grew up to command the Dutch Fleet.

The collections The first rooms of the museum chronicle the city's early history and its rise to prominence in trade and commerce. The displays include a wide selection of furniture, memorabilia and a map which illuminates each 25-year period of growth through the centuries. The main focus of the museum, however, is on the Golden Age and colonial expansion. Paintings and photos illustrate the growing welfare problems of the 19th and early 20th centuries, and a small collection of World War II relics shows how the Nazi occupation affected the city, whose population was ten per cent Jewish. Finally, be sure not to miss the portraits of the dapper Civic Guard, an armed civilian force formed in the late 14th century to police the city, which hang in the adjoining Schuttersgalerij.

HIGHLIGHTS

- *View of Amsterdam* (Cornelis Anthonisz, 1538), the oldest city map
- *The Meal of the 17 Guardsmen of Company H* (Cornelis Anthonisz, 1533), in the Schuttersgalerij
- *The First Steamship on the IJ* (Nicolaas Bauo, 1816)
- *Governesses at the Burgher Orphanage* (Adriaen Backer, 1683)
- *Girls from the Civic Orphanage* (Nicolaas van der Waay, 1880)
- Cartouches and gable stones at Sint Luciensteeg entrance
- Bell room

INFORMATION

- H5
- Kalverstraat 92, Nieuwezijds Voorburgwal 357, St Luciensteeg 27
- 5231822
- Mon–Fri 10–5, weekends 11–5. Closed 1 Jan, 30 Apr, 25 Dec
- David and Goliath Café (££)
- Tram 1, 2, 4, 5, 9, 16, 24, 25
- Very good
- Moderate
- Begijnhof (➤ 34), Koninklijk Paleis (➤ 36)
- Guided tours on request: telephone in advance

Top: Armour on display in the Amsterdams Historisch Museum

13

KONINKLIJK PALEIS

DID YOU KNOW?

- The state bought the palace in 1936 for f10 million
- The palace rests on 13,659 piles driven 18m into the ground
- It is 80m long and 56m wide
- The bell tower is 51m high

INFORMATION

- ✚ H5
- ✉ Dam
- ☎ 6248698
- 🕐 Jun–Aug Tue–Thu 1–4, other days 12:30–5 ; Sep–May phone for details. Closed public holidays and when the Queen is in residence
- 🚊 Tram 4, 9, 14, 16, 24, 25
- ♿ Good
- 🍴 Moderate
- ↔ Nieuwe Kerk (➤ 37), Amsterdams Historisch Museum (➤ 35), Begijnhof (➤ 34)

"*Don't be put off by the sober appearance of the exterior. The stern, heavy façade belies a lavishly decorated interior reminiscent of the power that Amsterdam enjoyed in its heyday.*"

Civic pride The Royal Palace was built at the height of the Golden Age, as a new town hall. Architect Jacob van Campen was commissioned to design the largest and grandest Stadhuis in Europe and its classical design was a startling progressive departure from the Dutch Renaissance style. The poet Constantyn Huygens called it 'the world's Eighth Wonder' and to this day it remains the city's only secular building erected on such grand scale. Note the astonishing wealth of decoration on the façade, with its numerous statues, elaborate pediment and huge cupola crowned by a galleon weathervane. Construction took seven years, during which time a heated argument developed as to whether a church tower for the Nieuwe Kerk should have priority over a town hall. The situation was rapidly resolved when the old town hall burnt down, and in 1655 the mayor moved into his new building.

Palatial splendour The town hall was transformed into a royal palace in 1808 after Napoleon made his brother Louis King of Holland. Today it serves as an occasional residence for Queen Beatrix, whose principal palace is in The Hague. Inside, be sure to see the sumptuous Burgerzaal (Citizen's Hall), running the length of the palace, with the entire eastern and western hemispheres mapped out on the floor, and the Tribunal. The latter was once the city's main courtroom, and condemned prisoners were taken from here to be hanged publicly in Dam Square.

NIEUWE KERK

"Considering its turbulent history, it is something of a miracle that Holland's magnificent national church has survived to this day. Should you get the chance to hear the organ, you are in for a real treat."

Not so new The 'New' Church actually dates from the 15th century, when Amsterdam was growing at such a rate that the 'Old' Church (Oude Kerk, ►40) was no longer sufficient. Construction started in 1408 but the church was several times destroyed by fire. After the 1578 Alteration (when Amsterdam officially became Protestant) and a further fire in 1645, the church was finally rebuilt and reconsecrated in 1648. It has no spire because, following years of fierce debate, the money designated for it was spent on the Royal Palace (►36). It does have one of the finest of Amsterdam's 42 historic church organs.

Famous names At the time of the Alteration (►12), Amsterdam's churches were largely stripped of their treasures, and the Nieuwe Kerk was no exception. The redundant altar space has since been filled with the tomb of Holland's most valiant naval hero, Admiral de Ruyter, one of a catalogue of household names from Dutch history, including poets P C Hooft and Joost van den Vondel, buried in the church. A window of 1650 shows the granting of the city's coat of arms by William IV. Another, by Otto Mengelberg, shows Wilhelmina at her inauguration in 1898, and marked her 40th year as Queen. The Nieuwe Kerk acquired its status of national church in the 19th century and Dutch monarchs have been inaugurated here, from William I in 1815 to Beatrix in 1980. Although it is no longer a place of worship, it holds regular exhibitions and organ recitals.

Top: tomb of Michiel de Ruyter. Above: the Nieuwe Kerk from Dam Square

HIGHLIGHTS

- Organ (Hans Schonat and Jacob Hagerbeer, 1650–73)
- Organ case (Jacob van Campen 1645)
- Pulpit (Albert Vinckenbrinck, 1649)
- Tomb of Admiral de Ruyter (Rombout Verhulst, 1681)

INFORMATION

- ✚ H5
- ✉ Dam
- ☎ 6268168
- ⓘ Variable
- 🍴 Nieuwe Café (££)
- 🚊 Tram 4, 9, 14, 16, 24, 25
- ♿ Good
- 🎨 Varies with exhibitions
- ↔ Koninklijk Paleis (►36)

37

15

BLOEMENMARKT

HIGHLIGHTS

- De Tuin bulb stand (opposite Singel 502) (➤ 71)
- Van Zoomeren cactus display (opposite Singel 526)
- Vazoplant pots and stands (opposite Singel 514)

INFORMATION

✚ H5
✉ Singel (between Muntplein and Koningsplein)
🕐 Mon–Sat 9–5
🚇 Muntplein
🚋 Tram 1, 2, 4, 5, 9, 14, 16, 24, 25
♿ Good
↔ Singel (➤ 33), Begijnhof (➤ 34), Amsterdams Historisch Museum (➤ 35)

Tulipa Whittalli *from Curtis's Botanical Magazine* c1795

"*Golden sunflowers, deep blue irises, delicately scented roses and row upon row of brightly packaged tulip bulbs... the barges of Amsterdam's fragrant flower market are always ablaze with colour and a feast for the senses whatever the season.***"**

Floating market During the 17th and 18th centuries there were approximately 20 floating markets in Amsterdam, at least two of which catered for the Dutch passion for tulips. Nurserymen would sail up the Amstel from their smallholdings and moor here to sell their wares directly from their boats. Today, the stalls at this, the city's only remaining floating market, still float, but they are permanently moored. Offering a vast variety of seasonal flowers, plants, pots, shrubs and herbs, they are supplied by the florists of Aalsmeer and the region around Haarlem (➤ 20), at the horticultural heart of Holland. With over 40,000 acres of the country devoted to bulb growing, it is easy to see why the Dutch are nicknamed 'the florists of Europe'.

Tulip mania Tulips were first spotted in Turkey by Dutch diplomats, who brought them back to Holland around 1600. Shortly afterwards, a Leiden botanist discovered ways of changing their shape and colour, and tulip cultivation rapidly became a national obsession. Prices soared, with single bulbs fetching up to f3,000 (an average worker's annual salary was f150). Some were even exchanged for houses, and an abundance of still-life paintings was produced to capture prize blooms on canvas. In 1637, the bubble burst, and many people lost entire fortunes. Prices are more realistic today and tulip bulbs are popular souvenirs; the Bloemenmarkt remains the best place to buy them.

PROSTUTIEZONE

"Amsterdam's Red Light District, bathed in a lurid red neon glow, with its scantily clad flesh, its gaping tourists, and its junkies and pickpockets, is one of the city's greatest attractions."

Sex for sale Sex is, and always has been, big business in Amsterdam. For centuries prostitutes have worked here, attracted by the port and the itinerant population of seamen. As early as the 15th century, Amsterdam was infamous as a centre of prostitution, and the lure of the Red Light District proves irresistible to most visitors to the city today. Crowds flock through the maze of narrow alleyways, past the ubiquitous sex shops, peep shows and suggestively named bars, while bored-looking prostitutes beckon from their pink-lit windows. But, believe it or not, there is more to the Red Light District than sex. Amongst the sleaziness, there are also some ordinary, welcoming cafés, bars and restaurants .

Hashish The Red Light District is also frequented by drug-dealers, and here you will find the great majority of Amsterdam's psychedelic, marijuana-selling 'smoking' coffee shops (►69). The Hash Marijuana Hemp Museum on Oudezijds Achterburgwal is the only museum in Europe tracing the history of hashish and the cannabis plant, and is located next to the world's only Cannabis Connoisseurs' Club.

Safety Remember that this is Amsterdam's main centre of drug-trafficking and prostitution, and exercise proper precautions. Watch your wallet, avoid eye contact with any undesirable characters, do not take photographs of prostitutes, and avoid poorly lit alleyways. Even though the evening is the liveliest time to visit, it is best not to wander around alone.

DID YOU KNOW?

- Possession of drugs is technically illegal but the authorities tolerate possession of up to 30g of soft drugs for personal use
- Drug-trafficking is not allowed, the existence of 'smoking' coffee shops is tolerated (►69)
- 30 per cent of hard-drug users in the city carry the AIDS virus
- Brothels were legalised in 1990
- Over half the prostitutes are foreign

INFORMATION

- ✚ H4–5
- ✉ Borders roughly denoted by Zeedijk (north), Kloveniersburgwal (east), Damstraat (south) and Warmoesstraat (west)
- 🍴 Restaurants, bars, cafés (£–£££)
- Ⓒ Centraal Station, Nieuwmarkt
- 🚃 Tram 4, 9, 16, 24, 25
- ⬌ Oude Kerk (►40), Museum Amstelkring (►41)

17

OUDE KERK

HIGHLIGHTS

- Great Organ (Vatermüller)
- Stained glass windows (Lambert van Noort, 1555)
- Carillon (F Hemony 1658)

INFORMATION

- ✚ H5
- ✉ Oudekerksplein 1
- ☎ 6258284
- ◷ Daily 1–5, except Sat 11–1. Closed 1 Jan, 30 Apr
- 🚋 Tram 4, 9, 16, 24, 25
- ♿ Good
- 💶 Moderate
- ↔ Prostutiezone (➤ 39), Museum Amstelkring (➤ 41)
- ❓ Frequent organ recitals and carillon concerts

The 18th-century Great Organ

❝Overlooked by prostitutes' windows and surrounded by the cafés, bars and sex shops of the frenetic Red Light District, the Old Church is an island of spiritual solace. The contrast is bizarre but typical of Amsterdam.**❞**

History Amsterdam's oldest church, dedicated to St Nicholas, the patron saint of seafarers, was built in 1306 to replace a wooden chapel which probably dated from the late 1200s. Over the centuries the church escaped the great fires which devastated so much of the city, and the imposing basilica you see today dates largely from the 14th century. Its graceful tower, added in 1565–67, contains one of the finest carillons in Holland. In the 16th century Jan Pieters Sweelinck, Holland's best-known composer, was organist here.

Miracle In the 14th century, Amsterdam became one of Europe's main pilgrimage centres, following a miracle. When a dying man regurgitated the bread he had received at communion, it was thrown on the fire, but miraculously would not burn. Today, thousands of Catholics still take part in the annual *Stille Omgang*, a silent nocturnal procession along the ancient pilgrim route to the church.

Sober interior The impressive, stark interior has a triple nave and elaborate vaulting. Three magnificent windows in the Lady Chapel survived the 16th-century Alteration, as did the finely carved choir-stools. In the 1960s some delicate 14th-century paintings were found behind layers of blue paint in the vaults. The tombstone of Rembrandt's first wife, Saskia van Uylenburg, is still in the church even though poverty drove him to sell her graveplot.

MUSEUM AMSTELKRING

❝One of Amsterdam's best-kept secrets – not only is this tiny museum one of the most surprising, it is also off the beaten tourist track, tucked away in a small, inconspicuous canal house on the edge of the Red Light District.❞

The Alteration In 1578, when the Roman Catholic city council was replaced by a Protestant one (►12), Roman Catholic churches were closed throughout the city. In 1661, while Catholic church services were still forbidden, a wealthy merchant called Jan Hartman built a residence on the Oudezijds Voorburgwal, and two adjoining houses in the Heintje Hoeckssteeg. He ran a sock shop on the ground floor, lived upstairs, let out the spare rooms in the buildings behind and cleverly converted the top two storeys of the canal house, and the attics of all three buildings, into a secret church.

Hidden church This 'schuilkerk' was just one of many clandestine churches which sprang up throughout the city, but it is the only one which has been completely preserved. It was saved from demolition in 1888 by a group of historians called the Amstelkring (Amstel 'circle'), who nicknamed the church 'Our Dear Lord in the Attic'. At the top of a series of increasingly steep staircases, to find a three-storey, galleried church is an awesome experience, with magnificent ecclesiastical statuary, silver, paintings and a collapsible altar. With seating for around 200 people and a huge organ, it is hard to believe that the services held here were really secret. Look out for the resident priest's tiny hidden bedroom under the stairs, and the confessional on the landing. The rest of the complex has been restored, and provides a taste of domestic life in the 17th century.

HIGHLIGHTS

- Church of 'Our Dear Lord in the Attic'
- Altar painting *The Baptism of Christ* (Jacob de Wit, 1716)
- Priest's bedroom
- Confessional
- Drawing room
- Kitchen

DID YOU KNOW?

- The altarpiece is one of three paintings by Jacob de Wit, designed to be interchangeable
- The church is still a consecrated place of worship

INFORMATION

- H4
- Oudezijds Voorburgwal 40
- 6246604
- Mon–Sat 10–5, Sun & public hols 1–5. Closed 1 Jan, 30 Apr
- Centraal Station
- Tram 4, 9, 16, 24, 25
- Centraal Station
- Museumboat stop 0
- None
- Moderate
- Prostutiezone (►39), Oude Kerk (►40)
- Classical concerts during winter

Top: 'Our Dear Lord in the Attic'

19

MUSEUM WILLET-HOLTHUYSEN

HIGHLIGHTS

- Blue Room
- Dining Room
- Porcelain and silver collections
- Kitchen
- Garden Room
- Garden

INFORMATION

- H5–6
- Herengracht 605
- 5231870
- Mon–Fri 10–5, weekends 11–5
- Waterlooplein
- Tram 4, 9, 14
- Museumboat stop 5
- None
- Moderate
- Herengracht (► 32), Magere Brug (► 45), Joods Historisch Museum (► 46)

"Behind the impressive façade of this gracious double-fronted mansion lies a sumptuously furnished patrician home with a delightful garden, a rare luxury in Amsterdam. Step inside and experience the high life."

Insight This beautifully preserved house on Herengracht, Amsterdam's most elegant canal (► 32), was built in 1687 for Jacob Hop, a wealthy member of the city council. It changed hands many times and eventually, in 1855, came into the possession of a glass merchant called Pieter Gerard Holthuysen. On his death, it became the home of his daughter Sandra and her husband, the art-collector Abraham Willet, and together they built up a valuable collection of glass, silver, ceramics and paintings. The couple bequeathed the house and its contents to the city in 1895, to be used as a museum. Initially it was visited so rarely that people used to joke that it was the best place for a gentleman to meet his mistress unobserved. However, following extensive restoration, the museum now provides a rare insight into life in the grand canal-houses in the 17th to 19th centuries.

Luxury and grandeur The rooms are lavishly decorated with inlaid wood, lacquered panelling and painted ceilings. Be sure to see the Blue Room, formerly the exclusive preserve of the gentlemen of the house, and the 17th-century kitchen with its original plumbing. Guests would be entertained to tea in the tiny, round Garden Room which, painted in the customary pale green, looks out over an immaculate French-style formal garden, lined with topiary and studded with statues. This is one of the city's few surviving 18th-century gardens – a jewel not to be missed.

Top: the Dining Room laid ready for dinner

STOELTIE DIAMONDS

"A tour here is sure to add extra sparkle to your city visit. There is no pressure to buy, but the allure of all those dazzling jewels could leave a gaping hole in your wallet."

Diamonds are forever Amsterdam's association with diamonds dates back to the 16th century, when Antwerp was taken by the Spanish and thousands of refugees fled north, including Jewish diamond-cutters and the city's most prosperous Jewish merchants. Amsterdam's guild controls prevented Jews from entering most other trades so they specialised in diamonds and soon established thriving diamond businesses, processing and dealing in the stones. By the 19th century, these were employing thousands of workers, and when vast fields of diamonds were discovered in South Africa in 1867, most of the stones were brought to Amsterdam to be cut, making Amsterdam the diamond capital of the world until World War II, when most of the city's Jewish workers were deported to concentration camps, never to return. As a result, Antwerp won back leadership of the world diamond market after the war, although diamonds from Amsterdam still have a reputation for quality and outstanding workmanship.

Tour There are 24 diamond-polishing factories in Amsterdam, many offering tours for groups and individuals. Stoeltie's tour lasts about 30 minutes, and includes a brief history of diamonds, their many industrial applications, how they are mined and the fine art of diamond production, a surprisingly grimy process considering the brilliant product. It is fascinating to watch the craftworkers at their benches, deftly cutting, polishing, sorting and setting the glittering gems and to learn about the 'four Cs' – colour, clarity, cut and carat weight – which determine the value of the stone, should you wish to buy.

DID YOU KNOW?

- The first records of Amsterdam's diamond industry date from 1586
- At its peak, it employed over 10,000 workers
- Only 20 per cent of diamonds become gemstones for jewellery
- The world's largest-ever cut diamond, the Cullinan I ('Star of Africa') weighs 530 carats. The world's smallest-ever cut diamond has 57 facets and weighs 0.0012 carats. Both were processed in Amsterdam
- The General Dutch Diamond Workers Union, founded in 1894, was the first union in the world to achieve an eight-hour working day

INFORMATION

- ✠ H5
- ✉ Wagenstraat 13–17
- ☎ 6237601
- 🕐 Daily 9–5
- 🚇 Waterlooplein
- 🚊 Tram 4, 9, 14
- ♿ Very good
- 🎫 Free
- ↔ Museum Willet-Holthuysen (➤ 42)

Top: working on diamonds

43

MUSEUM HET REMBRANDTHUIS

HIGHLIGHTS

- Self-portrait with a Surprised Expression
- Jan Six
- Five Studies of the Head of Saskia and One of an Older Woman
- View of Amsterdam
- Christ Shown to the People

INFORMATION

- ✚ H5
- ✉ Jodenbreestraat 4–6
- ☎ 6249486
- ◷ Mon–Sat 10–5, Sun & public hols 1–5. Closed 1 Jan
- Ⓜ Nieuwmarkt, Waterlooplein
- 🚋 Tram 9, 14
- 🚢 Museumboat stop 5
- ♿ Few
- 💶 Moderate
- ↔ Joods Historisch Museum (➤ 46), Museum Willet-Holthuysen (➤ 42)
- ❓ Brief film of Rembrandt's life

Below: Self-portrait with Saskia *Rembrandt, 1636*

" *The lack of Rembrandt's own belongings in this intimate house is more than compensated for by a virtually complete collection of his etchings. They are fascinating, whether or not you are an art enthusiast.* **"**

From riches to rags Rembrandt spent the happiest and most successful years of his life in this red-shuttered canal house, and produced many of his most famous paintings and prints here. Thanks to his wife, the wealthy heiress Saskia van Uylenburg, the up-and-coming young artist had been introduced to Amsterdam's patrician class and commissions for portraits had poured in. He had rapidly become an esteemed painter, and in 1639 bought this large, three-storey house as a symbol of his new-found respectability. However, Saskia's tragic, untimely death in 1642 marked the start of Rembrandt's financial decline. His work became unfashionable, and in 1656 he was declared bankrupt. The house and most of his possessions were sold in 1660, and he eventually died a pauper (➤ 30).

Funny faces It is a strange experience to see 260 of the 280 etchings ascribed to Rembrandt in the very surroundings in which they were created. His achievements in etching were as important as those in his painting, since it was thanks to his mastery in this medium that it was recognised as an art form for the first time. Four of his copper etching plates are on display on the ground floor, together with an exhibition on traditional etching techniques, and a series of biblical illustrations. Visit the first floor too, where Rembrandt's studies of street figures are hung alongside some highly entertaining self-portraits in various guises, and some mirror-images of himself pulling faces.

MAGERE BRUG

" *The 'Skinny Bridge' – a traditional double-leaf Dutch drawbridge – is a much-loved city landmark, and one of the most photographed sights in Amsterdam. Visit at night, when it is lit by strings of enchanting fairy lights.* **"**

Skinny sisters Of Amsterdam's 1,200 or so bridges, the Magere Brug is, without doubt, the best known. Situated on the Amstel river (from which the city takes its name), the wooden bridge you see today is a 20th-century replica of the original 17th-century drawbridge. Tradition has it that, in 1670, a simple footbridge was built by two elderly sisters named *Mager* (meaning 'skinny'), who lived on one side of the Amstel and wanted easy access to their carriage and horses, stabled on the other bank. It seems more likely, however, that the bridge took its name from its narrow girth. In 1772 it was widened and became a double drawbridge, enabling ships of heavy tonnage to sail up the Amstel from the IJ.

City uproar In 1929 the city council started discussing whether to demolish the old frame which had rotted. It was to be replaced with an electrically operated bridge. This caused an outcry amongst the people of Amsterdam who voted overwhelmingly for the original wooden bridge to be saved.

The present bridge was erected in 1969, and is made of African azobe wood. Its mechanical drive was installed in 1994. Every now and then, you can watch the bridge master raising the bridge to let boats through. He then cycles hastily upstream to open the Amstel and Hoge sluice gates, only to remount his bike and repeat the whole procedure.

DID YOU KNOW?

- 63,000 boats pass under the bridge each year
- Rebuilding in 1969 cost f140,000
- There are 60 drawbridges in Amsterdam

INFORMATION

- ✚ H6
- ✉ Amstel
- Ⓜ Waterlooplein
- 🚊 Tram 4, 9, 14
- 🚢 Museumboat stop 5
- ↔ Museum Willet-Holthuysen (► 42), Joods Historisch Museum (► 46)

Top: the Magere Brug, all lit up at night

23

JOODS HISTORISCH MUSEUM

HIGHLIGHTS

- Grote Schul (Great Synagogue, 1671)
- Holy Ark (1791)
- Haggadah Manuscript (1734)

DID YOU KNOW?

- 1597 First Jew gained Dutch citizenship
- 1602 Judaism first practised openly here
- 1671 The Grote Schul became the first synagogue in Western Europe
- 80 per cent of Dutch Jews were exterminated in World War II
- Restoration of the synagogues cost over f13 million

INFORMATION

- ✚ H5
- ✉ Jonas Daniel Meijerplein 2–4
- ☎ 6269945
- 🕐 Daily 11–5. Closed Yom Kippur
- 🍴 Café (££)
- Ⓜ Waterlooplein
- 🚋 Tram 9, 14
- 🚢 Museumboat stop 5
- ♿ Very good
- 💷 Moderate
- ↔ Museum het Rembrandthuis (➤ 44), Museum Willet-Holthuysen (➤ 42), Magere Brug (➤ 45)
- ❓ Bookshop

Top: the Great Synagogue

"*A remarkable exhibition devoted to Judaism and the story of Jewish settlement in Amsterdam, of interest to Jews and Gentiles alike. For me, the most memorable and poignant part portrays the horrors of the Holocaust.***"**

Reconstruction Located in the heart of what used to be a Jewish neighbourhood, this massive complex of four synagogues forms the largest and most important Jewish museum outside Israel. The buildings lay in ruins for many years after World War II, and have only recently been painstakingly reconstructed as a monument to the strength of the Jewish faith, and to the suffering of the Jewish people under the Nazis.

Historical exhibits The New Synagogue (1752) gives a lengthy, detailed history of Zionism, with displays of religious artefacts. The Great Synagogue (1671) is of more general interest, defining the role of the Jewish community in Amsterdam's trade and industry. Downstairs is a chilling exhibition from the war years and a moving collection by Jewish painters, including a series entitled *Life? or Theatre?* by Charlotte Salomon, who died in Auschwitz aged 26.

'The Dockworker' The Nazis occupied Amsterdam in May 1940, and immediately began to persecute the Jewish population. In February 1941, 400 Jews were gathered outside the Great Synagogue by the SS, herded into trucks and taken away. This triggered the 'February Strike', a general strike led by dockers. Though suppressed after only two days, it was Amsterdam's first open revolt against Nazism, and gave impetus to the resistance movement. Every 25 February, a ceremony at Andriessen's statue 'The Dockworker' commemorates the strike.

NEDERLANDS SCHEEPVAART MUSEUM

"*Even resolute landlubbers will enjoy this maritime museum. It brings the country's glorious seafaring past to life in spectacular style, with full-size boats and hundreds of models. Children love it.***"**

Admiralty storehouse The vast classical building (1656) which now houses the Maritime Museum was formerly the Dutch Admiralty's central store. Here the East India Company would load their ships prior to the eight-month journey to Jakarta, headquarters of the VOC in Indonesia (▶ 12). In 1973, the arsenal was converted into this museum, which boasts the largest collection of boats in the world.

Voyages of discovery An ancient dug-out, a re-created section of a destroyer, schooners and luxury liners depict Holland's remarkable maritime history. Children can peer through periscopes and operate a radar cabin, while parents marvel at some 500 magnificent model ships and study the charts, instruments, weapons, maps and globes from the great age of exploration. Don't miss the first-ever sea atlas, the mid-16th century three-masted ship model, or the beautiful royal sloop – the 'golden coach on water' – last used in 1962 for Queen Juliana's silver wedding celebrations.

The *Amsterdam* The highlight of the museum is moored alongside – the square-rigger *Amsterdam*, a replica of the 18th-century Dutch East Indiaman which sank during her maiden voyage off the English coast in 1749. A vivid multimedia film 'Voyage to the East Indies' (rather gory for children) is shown, and in summer, actors become bawdy 'sailors', firing cannons, swabbing the decks, loading cargo and enacting daily burials at sea.

HIGHLIGHTS

- The *Amsterdam*
- Royal sloop
- Blaue's World Atlas (Room 1)
- First printed map of Amsterdam (Room 1)
- Three-masted ship (Room 2)
- Wartime exhibits (Rooms 21–24)

INFORMATION

- ✚ J5
- ✉ Kattenburgerplein 1
- ☎ 5232222
- 🕐 Tue–Sat 10–5, Sun & hols 12–5. (Also Mon 10–5 in summer). Closed 1 Jan. Crew on board *Amsterdam* in summer Mon–Sat 10:30–4:15, Sun 12:30–4:15
- 🍴 Café (£)
- 🚌 Bus 22, 28
- 🚋 Artis Express from Centraal Station
- ⛴ Museumboat stop 6
- ♿ Very good
- 💰 Expensive
- 🔄 Artis Zoo (▶ 59), Hortus Botanicus (▶ 58)
- ❓ Souvenir and book shop, model-boat kit shop Thu and Fri only, multimedia theatre

Top: the ornate stern of the replica of the Amsterdam

25

TROPENMUSEUM

INFORMATION

- ✚ K6
- ✉ Linnaeusstraat 2
- ☎ 5688215. Children's Museum ☎ 5688233
- 🕐 Mon–Fri 10–5, weekends and hols 12–5. Closed 1 Jan, 30 Apr, 5 May, 25 Dec. Children's Museum 🕐 Wed afternoons and weekends; and Mon–Fri during school holidays
- 🍴 Café and restaurant 'World Buffet'
- 🚊 Tram 9, 14
- ♿ Very good
- 💲 Expensive
- ↔ Artis Zoo (▶ 59), Hortus Botanicus (▶ 58)
- ❓ Soeterijn Theatre. Shop ☎ 5688233 for further information

Top: statue of a Hindu goddess in the Tropenmuseum

" *There is no need to travel round the world anymore! Come to this extra-ordinary Tropical Museum instead. Its authentic reconstructions of street scenes evoke the everyday life of people in tropical regions all over the world.* **"**

Foundations In 1859, Frederik Willem van Eeden, a member of the Dutch Society for the Promotion of Industry, was asked to establish a collection of objects from the Dutch colonies 'for the instruction and amusement of the Dutch people'. The collection started with a simple bow, arrows and quiver from Borneo and a lacquer waterscoop from Palembang, but thereafter it expanded at a staggering rate, as did the number of visitors. In the 1920s a palatial building, the Colonial Institute, was constructed to house the collection, and adorned with stone friezes to reflect Holland's imperial achievements. In the 1970s, there was a shift in emphasis away from the glories of colonialism towards Third World problems.

Another world The precious collections are not displayed in glass cases, but instead are set out in lifelike settings, amid evocative sounds, photographs and slide presentations, enabling visitors to step into other continents: explore a Bombay slum, feel the fabrics in an Arabian souk, have a rest in a Nigerian bar, contemplate in a Hindu temple, or listen to the sounds of Latin America in a local café. The museum's Ekeko restaurant offers a 'World Buffet' and there is also a theatre, the Soeterijn, where visiting performers put on non-Western music, theatre and dance in the evenings. During the day, Children's Museum activities provide an insight into other cultures. Beside the Museum is the Oosterpark, a pleasant green space.

AMSTERDAM's
best

CANALS & WATERWAYS

See Top 25 sights for:
HERENGRACHT (➤ 32)
PRINSENGRACHT (➤ 29)
SINGEL (➤ 33)

Sunken booty

The canals receive many of the city's unwanted items. Over 100 million litres of sludge and rubbish are removed annually by a fleet of ten council boats: six for recovering floating refuse, one for retrieving bikes (about 10,000 a year) and three dredgers. Amongst the 'treasures' they find are stolen wallets, parking metres, cars with failed handbrakes, and even an occasional corpse.

AMSTEL
The river is a busy commercial thoroughfare, with barges carrying goods to and from the port. Its sturdy 18th-century wooden sluice gates are closed four times a week. This enables fresh water from the IJmeer to flow into the canal network.
✚ H5–6, 9–10, J6–9 🚊 Tram 4, 9, 14, 16, 24, 25

AMSTERDAM–RHINE CANAL
Amsterdam's longest waterway stretches from the IJ to Switzerland.
✚ M5–6, N6–7 🚌 Bus 37, 220, 245

BLAUWBURGWAL
Amsterdam's shortest canal, between Singel and Herengracht.
✚ H4 🚊 Tram 1, 2, 5, 13, 17

BLOEMGRACHT AND EGELANTIERSGRACHT
These intimate, narrow thoroughfares in the Jordaan, lined with colourful small boats, provide a retreat from the hustle and bustle of the city centre.
✚ G4–5 🚊 Tram 13, 14, 17

BROUWERSGRACHT
Also in the Jordaan, the Brouwersgracht owes its name to the many breweries established here in the 16th and 17th centuries. The houseboats and old warehouses (once used to store barley but today converted into luxury apartments) make this leafy canal particularly photogenic.
✚ G–H4 🚉 Centraal Station

The junction of the Keizersgracht and the Reguliersgracht

GROENBURGWAL

This idyllic, picturesque canal near the Stopera was Monet's favourite.

➕ H5 🚇 Nieuwmarkt

THE IJ

Amsterdam is situated on precariously low-lying ground at the confluence of the IJ and Amstel rivers. During Amsterdam's heyday in the 17th century, most maritime activity was centred on the IJ and along Prins Hendrikkade, where the old warehouses were crammed with spices and other exotic produce from the East. Since 1876 however, access to the sea has been via the North Sea Canal, and the working docks are now to the west. There is little activity on the IJ today apart from a few passenger ships and the free shuttle ferry to Amsterdam Noord.

➕ F1–N6 🚇 Centraal Station

KEIZERSGRACHT

Together with Prinsengracht and Heren-gracht, this broad, elegant canal, built in 1612 and named Emperor's Canal after Emperor Maximilian I, completes the Grachtengordel (Canal Ring) – the trio of concentric city-centre canals, that, intersected by a series of narrower, radial waterways, make a cobweb of water across the city.

➕ G4–6, H6 🚋 Tram 1, 2, 5, 13, 14, 16, 17, 24, 25

A bridge over the Keizersgracht

LEIDSEGRACHT

One of the most exclusive addresses in town.

➕ G5–6 🚋 Tram 1, 2, 5

LOOIERSGRACHT

In the 17th century, the main industry in the Jordaan was tanning, hence the name Tanner's Canal. Many of the surrounding streets are named after the animals whose pelts were used such as Hazenstraat (Hare Street), Reestraat (Deer Street) and Wolven-straat (Wolf Street).

➕ G5 🚋 Tram 7, 10

OUDEZIJDS ACHTERBURGWAL AND OUDEZIJDS VOORBURGWAL

In contrast to most of Amsterdam's canals, which are peaceful and romantic, the Oudezijds Achterburgwal and Oudezijds Voorburgwal are lined with glaring, neon-lit bars and sex shops.

➕ H4–5 🚋 Tram 4, 9, 16, 24, 25

REGULIERSGRACHT

Seven bridges cross the water here in quick succession. They are best viewed from the water at night, when they are lit by strings of fairy lights.

➕ H6 🚋 Tram 4, 16, 24, 25

Old docklands

Amsterdam ranks among the world's 15 busiest ports, handling 45 million tonnes per year. It is Nissan's European distribution centre and the world's largest cocoa port. The city's old harbour has been consumed by developers, but for a taste of its former glory, head to the Scheepvaart Museum (➤ 47) in the Eastern Islands, or to the Western Islands, where the carefully restored 17th-century warehouses, cluttered wharfs and nautical street names (Sailmaker Street, Rope Factory Street) offer an unspoilt glimpse of old Amsterdam off the tourist beat (➕ G3–H3 ✉ north of the railway between Wester-Kanal and Westerdoksdijk).

DISTRICTS

See Top 25 sights for
PROSTUTIEZONE (▶39)

A typically ornate gable

CHINATOWN
Europe's largest Chinese community earns part of its living from the numerous Chinese restaurants around Nieuwmarkt.
➕ H5 🚇 Nieuwmarkt

JODENHOEK
Jewish refugees first came here in the 16th century and settled on the cheap, marshy land southeast of Nieuwmarkt and bordered by the Amstel. Almost the entire district was razed to the ground at the end of World War II, leaving only a few synagogues (▶46) and diamond factories as legacy of a once-thriving community.
➕ H–J5 🚇 Waterlooplein

DE JORDAAN
This popular, bohemian quarter with its labyrinth of picturesque canals, narrow streets, trendy shops, cafés and restaurants, was once a boggy meadow alongside Prinsengracht. It became a slum area in the 17th century, and later a more respectable working-class district. The name is believed to come from the French *jardin*, for garden.
➕ G4 🚋 Tram 3, 10, 13, 14, 17

Grachtengordel (Canal Ring)
The buildings along the web of canals around the medieval city centre are supported on thousands of wooden piles, to stop them from sinking. Constructed as part of a massive 17th-century expansion project the immaculate patrician mansions along Prinsengracht, Keizersgracht and Herengracht look almost like a toy town in a child's picture book, with their trim brickwork and characterful gables. The best way to enjoy their architectural details is from the water (▶19).

DE PIJP
This lively, multi-cultural area was once one of Amsterdam's most attractive working-class districts outside the Grachtengordel. The bustling Albert Cuypmarkt takes place daily (▶53), and there are several diamond-cutting workshops.
➕ H7 🚋 Tram 4, 16, 24, 25

PLANTAGE
The 'Plantation' became one of Amsterdam's first suburbs in 1848. Before that, this popular and leafy residential area was parkland.
➕ J5–6 🚋 Tram 9, 14

ZEEDIJK
Once the sea wall of the early maritime settlement and until recently the haunt of sailors and shady characters, this area on the fringe of the Red Light District boasts superb bars and restaurants.
➕ H4–5 🚇 Centraal Station 🚋 Tram 1, 2, 4, 5, 9, 13, 16, 17, 24, 25

MARKETS

See Top 25 sights for
BLOEMENMARKT (▶ 38)

ALBERT CUYPMARKT
Amsterdam's best-known, cheapest general market, named after a Dutch landscape artist, attracts some 20,000 bargain hunters on busy days.
➕ H7 ✉ Albert Cuypstraat ⏰ Mon–Sat 10–5 🚊 Tram 4, 16, 24, 25

NOORDERMARKT
For a taste of the Jordaan district, head for the lively square surrounding the Noorderkerk. On Monday morning visit the *Lapjesmarkt* textile and secondhand clothing market, and on Saturday try the *Boerenmarkt* for organically grown fresh produce, crafts and birds.
➕ G4 ✉ Noordermarkt ⏰ Mon, Sat 9–1 🚌 Bus 18, 22, 44

OUDEMANHUISPOORT
Antiquarian bookshops in an 18th-century arcade.
➕ H5 ✉ Oudemanhuispoort ⏰ Mon–Sat 10–4 🚊 Tram 4, 9, 16, 24, 25

POSTZEGELMARKT
A specialist market for stamps, coins and medals.
➕ H4–5 ✉ 280 Nieuwezijds Voorburgwal ⏰ Wed, Sat 1–4 🚊 Tram 1, 2, 5

ROMMELMARKT
A treasure trove of bric-à-brac. The word *rommel* means rummage.
➕ G5 ✉ Looiersgracht 38 ⏰ Sat–Thu 10–5 🚊 Tram 7, 10

WATERLOOPLEIN FLEAMARKET
Amsterdam's liveliest market, full of funky clothes, curiosities and 'antique' junk. Beware pickpockets.
➕ H5 ✉ Waterlooplein ⏰ Mon–Fri 9–5, Sat 8:30–5:30 🚇 Waterlooplein

ZWARTE MARKT
This huge indoor fleamarket outside Amsterdam (reputedly Europe's largest) has an Eastern Market overflowing with oriental merchandise.
➕ Off map to northwest ✉ Industriegebied aan de Buitenlandenden, Beverwijk-Oost ⏰ Sat 7–5, Sun (Eastern Market only) 8–6 🚉 Beverwijk-Oost

Markets
Amsterdam still resembles a collection of small villages, with every district having its own local market. The daily general markets at Ten Katestraat (Kinkerstraat) (➕ F5–6) and Dapperstraat (➕ K6) are particularly good for fruit and vegetables, and there is a flower market at Amstelveld (➕ H6) every Monday morning. Sunday art markets are held at Spui (➕ G–H5) and Thorbeckeplein (➕ H6) and you can often pick up a bargain at the Nieuwmarkt antiques market (➕ H5) on Sundays in summer.

Albert Cuypstraat market

BRIDGES, BUILDINGS & MONUMENTS

Bridges

No other city in the world has so many bridges. The majority are single or triple-arched hump-backed bridges made of brick and stone with simple cast-iron railings. The oldest bridge is the Torensluis (1648), and the best example of a traditional Dutch drawbridge is the Magere Brug (Skinny Bridge ➤ 45). The cast-iron Blauwbrug (Blue Bridge, 1874) is one of the most traditional (inspired by the Pont Alexandre III in Paris), whereas the 20th-century Waals Eilandsgracht bridge, with its triangular and trapezoidal arches, is the most modernistic.

99 Rokin, a modern interpretation of a canalside house

> **See Top 25 for**
> **ANNE FRANK STATUE, WESTERKERK (➤ 30)**
> **HET HOUTEN HUYS, BEGIJNHOF (➤ 34)**
> **JOODS HISTORISCH MUSEUM (➤ 46)**
> **KONINKLIJK PALEIS (➤ 36)**
> **LEIDSEPLEIN (AMERICAN HOTEL) (➤ 27)**
> **MAGERE BRUG (➤ 45)**

BEURS VAN BERLAGE

Designed by Hendrik Berlage, and now hailed as an early modernist masterpiece, the former stock exchange provoked outrage when it opened in 1903. It is now used as a concert hall (➤ 78).

➕ H4–5 ✉ Damrak 213–279 ☎ 6265257 🕐 Daily 9–5 for exhibitions 🍴 Café Ranieri (££) 🚊 Tram 4, 9, 16, 24, 25

CENTRAAL STATION

Many travellers get their first glimpse of Amsterdam's architectural wonders at P J H Cuyper's vast neo-classical station (1889), standing defiantly with its back to the River IJ.

➕ H4 ✉ Stationsplein ☎ 06/9292 🚇 Centraal Station

CONCERTGEBOUW

The orchestra and main concert hall of this elaborate Neo-Renaissance building have been renowned worldwide ever since its inaugural concert in 1888.

➕ G7 ✉ Concertgebouwplein 2–6 ☎ 6754411 🕐 Box office Mon–Sat 10–7 🚊 Tram 3, 5, 12, 16

ENTREPOTDOK

The old warehouses at Entrepotdok have been converted into offices and expensive apartments.

➕ J–L5 ✉ Entrepotdok 🚌 Bus 22

GREENPEACE HEADQUARTERS

This pragmatic city seems an appropriate home for the world's head office of Greenpeace, which occupies a remarkable *Jugendstil* (art nouveau) building (1905).

➕ G4 ✉ Keizersgracht 174 🚊 Tram 13, 14, 17

KERWIN DUINMEYER MONUMENT

Kerwin was a 15-year-old black youth who was stabbed to death in Amsterdam in 1983. It was the first time since World War II that someone had been killed in the city because of their race. His statue stands in the Vondelpark as a symbol of the Dutch fight against racism.

➕ F6 ✉ Vondelpark (Jacob Obrechtstraat exit) 🚊 Tram 2, 3, 5, 12

'T LIEVERDJE

In the '60s this little bronze statue of a boy, which stands so innocently in the middle of the square, became a symbol of the *Provo* movement, and rallying point of frequent anti-establishment demonstrations. The name means 'Little Darling'.

➕ G5 ✉ Spui 🚋 Tram 1, 2, 5

MUNTTOREN

The tower of the former Mint was part of the southern gateway to the medieval city.

➕ H5 ✉ Muntplein
🚋 Tram 4, 9, 14, 16, 24, 25

MUZIEK THEATER (STOPERA)

Amsterdam's new theatre for opera and dance is known as the Stopera, or less attractively, the 'false teeth' because of its white marble panelling and red brick roof. The complex includes the uninspiring buildings of the new town hall, and the design caused great controversy when it was built in 1986.

➕ H5 ✉ Waterlooplein
22 Ⓜ Waterlooplein

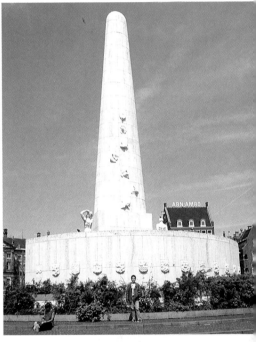

NATIONAL MONUMENT

The 22m obelisk in Dam Square contains soil from all the Dutch provinces and former colonies. Every year on 4 May, the Queen lays a wreath here.

➕ H5 ✉ Dam 🚋 Tram 4, 9, 14, 16, 24, 25

National Monument in Dam Square, in memory of World War II victims

SCHEEPVAART-HUIS

The peculiarly tapered Maritime House, encrusted with marine decoration, suggests the bow of an approaching ship. Commissioned by seven shipping companies in 1912, it represents one of most impressive examples of the architecture of the Amsterdam School.

➕ H5–J5 ✉ Prins Hendrikkade 108–111 🚌 Bus 22

SCHREIERSTOREN

The 'Weeping Tower' was where tearful (*schreien*) wives and girlfriends waved farewell to their seafaring menfolk. They had good reason to weep: in the 18th century, voyages took up to four years and many sailors died.

➕ H4 ✉ Prins Hendrikkade 94–95 Ⓜ Centraal Station

Homo Monument

One of the city's more controversial sculptures is the *Homo Monument* (1987) by Karin Daan, on the corner of Westermarkt and Keizersgracht. Consisting of three pink triangles, the sign homosexuals were forced to wear during the German Occupation, it commemorates all those who have been persecuted because of their homosexuality.

55

MUSEUMS & GALLERIES

Canal-house museums

The grand 17th-century canal house Museum van Loon (Keizersgracht 672), has an impressive family portrait gallery. The Theatermuseum (Herengracht 168) and the Bible Museum (Herengracht 366), with its priceless religious artefacts, are also in beautiful houses whose interiors alone warrant a visit.

A mug of Heineken

Museum passes

If you intend to visit several museums and galleries, buy a *Museumskaart* from the VVV for f47,50, granting you free entry into over 400 museums throughout Holland for one year. The *Amsterdam Culture & Leisure Pass* also offers various discounts, and only costs f29,90.

HEINEKEN BROUWERIJ
Free tastings of the world's best-known brand of Dutch beer are offered at the end of a comprehensive tour of Heineken's first brewery.
✚ H6 ✉ Stadhouderskade 78 ☎ 5239666 🕐 Guided tours (18 years and over only): Mon–Fri 9:30 and 11. Also Jun–mid Sep 1 and 2:30; Jul and Aug noon and 2 🚋 Tram 6, 7, 10, 16, 24, 25 ♿ Few (phone in advance) 💲 Cheap

MUSEUM AVIODOME
The National Aeronautics and Space Travel Museum has 25 aircraft from 1903 to 1954.
✚ X12 ✉ Westelijke Randweg 1, Schiphol-Centrum ☎ 6041521 🕐 Apr–Sep 10–5, Oct–Mar Tue–Fri 10–5, weekends 12–5. Closed 1 Jan, 25 and 31 Dec 🚉 Schiphol ♿ Good 💲 Moderate

SIX COLLECTION
Apply at the Rijksmuseum for a letter of introduction to visit this private collection of Dutch paintings. Its greatest treasure is Rembrandt's *Portrait of Jan Six*.
✚ H6 ✉ Amstel 218 ☎ 6732121 🕐 Guided tours only: Mon, Wed, Fri 10 and 11AM 🚋 Tram 4, 9, 14 ♿ None 💲 Free

VERZETSMUSEUM (RESISTANCE MUSEUM)
Rare wartime memorabilia and a fascinating summary of the Dutch resistance during World War II, housed in a former synagogue.
✚ H–J8 ✉ Lekstraat 63 ☎ 6449797 🕐 Tue–Fri 10–5, weekends 1–5. Closed 1 Jan, 30 Apr, 25 Dec 🚋 Tram 4, 12, 25 ♿ Good 💲 Cheap

WERF'T KROMHOUT MUSEUM
One of the city's few remaining working shipyards, this 18th-century wharf is used for restoring antique vessels, and is open to visitors as a museum in working hours.
✚ K5 ✉ Hoogte Kadijk 147 ☎ 6276777 🕐 Mon–Fri 10–4. Closed weekends, public hols 🚌 Bus 22, 28 ♿ Few 💲 Cheap

PLACES OF WORSHIP

See Top 25 sights for
MUSEUM AMSTELKRING (► 41)
NIEUWE KERK (► 37)
OUDE KERK (► 40)
WESTERKERK (► 30)

AMSTELKERK
Squat and wooden, this Calvinist church (1670) was originally meant to be a temporary structure while funds were raised for a larger building elsewhere.
✚ H6 ✉ Amstelveld ☎ 6238138 ⊘ Closed to public
🚋 Tram 4

FRANCISCUS XAVERIUSKERK
This splendid neo-Gothic church is often dubbed 'De Krijtberg' ('Chalk hill'), because it is built on the site of a former chalk merchant's house.
✚ G5 ✉ Singel 442–448 ☎ 6231923 ⊘ Services only
🚋 Tram 1, 2, 5

NOORDERKERK
An austere church, the first in Amsterdam to be constructed in the shape of a Greek cross. It was built in 1620–23 for the Protestant workers in the Jordaan district, and is still well attended.
✚ G4 ✉ Noordermarkt 44–48 ☎ 6266436 ⊘ Mar–Nov, Sat 11–1, and services 🚋 Tram 3, 10, 13, 14, 17

PORTUGUESE SYNAGOGUE
Holland's finest synagogue, one of the first of any size to be built in Western Europe. It is remarkable that this imposing building escaped destruction in World War II.
✚ J5 ✉ 🚇 Mr Visserplein 3 ☎ 6245351 ⊘ Sun–Fri 10–4 (closes two hours before sunset on Fri). Closed Jewish holidays 🍴 Sun 10–noon Ⓜ Waterlooplein

SINT NICOLAASKERK
Amsterdam's main Roman Catholic church (1888) and one of many Dutch churches named after St Nicholas, the patron saint of sailors. St Nicholas is also Sinterklaas (see panel).
✚ H4 ✉ Prins Hendrikkade 73 ☎ 6248749 ⊘ Mon–Sat 11–4 🍴 Services 🚋 Tram 1, 2, 4, 5, 9

ZUIDERKERK
Holland's first Protestant church (1614) and indisputably one of the city's most beautiful. Its designer, Hendrick de Keyser, lies buried within. The distinctive 80m-high tower affords spectacular views of the Nieuwmarkt district.
✚ H5 ✉ Zuiderkerkhof 72 ☎ 6222962 ⊘ Mon–Wed & Fri 12–5, Thu 12–8 Ⓜ Nieuwmarkt

Zuiderkerk

Sinterklaas
St Nicholas, or *Sinterklaas*, pays an early visit to the city each year on the second or third Saturday of November. Accompanied by *Zwarte Piet* (Black Peter), he arrives by boat near St Nicholaaskerk and distributes gingerbread to children, then receives the keys to the city from the mayor on Dam Square. On 5 December (*Sinterklaasavond* or Pakjesavond) he comes during the night with sacks of presents for the sleeping children.

PARKS & GARDENS

See Top 25 sights for
OOSTERPARK, TROPENMUSEUM (➤ 48)
VONDELPARK (➤ 24)

Hortus Botanicus

Laid out in 1682, the botanical gardens were originally sponsored by the VOC (➤ 12), whose members brought back plants and seeds from all corners of the earth, to be grown and studied by doctors and apothecaries here. One such plant – a coffee tree – given to Louis XIV of France and cultivated in his American colonies, was the ancestor of the Brazilian coffee plantations. Likewise, the production of palm oil in Indonesia is due to plants initially cultivated here.

Vondelpark

AMSTELPARK

A formal rose garden and a rhododendron valley are two of many seasonal spectacles at this magnificent park, created in 1972 for an international horticultural exhibition. It also offers pony rides, mini-golf, a children's farm, the Rieker windmill (➤ 60) and other attractions. There is a special walk for blind people and in summer you can tour the park in a miniature train.

➕ H9–10   ⏰ Dawn–dusk   🍴 Restaurant and café (££)   🚌 Bus 69, 148, 169

AMSTERDAMSE BOS

Amsterdam's largest park was built on the polders in the 1930s as part of a job creation scheme. It is a favourite family destination at weekends whatever the season – in winter, there is tobogganing and skating; in summer swimming, sailing and cycling. A leisurely tram ride can be taken through the park in colourful antique trolleycars from various European cities.

➕ C–E10   ⏰ Always open   🍴 Open-air pancake restaurant and café (££)   🚌 Bus 170, 171, 172

HORTUS BOTANICUS

With over 6,000 plant species, Holland's oldest garden boasts one of the largest botanical collections in the world. It has spectacular tropical greenhouses, a medicinal herb garden, and a monumental cycad which, at 400 years old, is reputed to be the world's oldest potted plant.

➕ J5   ✉ Plantage Middenlaan 2   ☎ 6258411   ⏰ Apr–Sep, Mon–Fri 9–5, weekends 11–5; Oct–Mar, Mon–Fri 9–4, weekends 11–4   🍴 Café (£)   🚊 Tram 7, 9, 14   ♿ Good   💶 Moderate

SARPHATI PARK

Enjoy a picnic bought at nearby Albert Cuypmarkt (➤ 53) in this tiny green oasis dedicated to the 19th-century Jewish doctor and city benefactor, Samuel Sarphati.

➕ H7   ⏰ 9–dusk   🚊 Tram 3, 4, 16, 24, 25

ATTRACTIONS FOR CHILDREN

ARTIS ZOO (NATURA ARTIS MAGISTRA)
The complex includes museums, Europe's biggest aquarium, and the Planetarium (hourly shows).
➕ JK5–6 ✉ Plantage Kerklaan 38–40 ☎ 6231836 🕐 Daily 9–5 🍴 Restaurant and café 🚊 Tram 7, 9, 14. Artis Express boat from Centraal Station ♿ Good 💶 Very expensive

DE DIERENPIJP
A children's farm at the heart of the city.
➕ H7 ✉ Lizzy Ansinghstraat 82 ☎ 6648303 🕐 Wed–Mon 1–5 🚊 Tram 24, 25 ♿ Few 💶 Cheap

DE KRAKELING THEATER
Mime and puppet shows, some for under-12s, others for over-12s.
➕ G5 ✉ Nieuwe Passeerderstraat 1 ☎ 6253284 🕐 Shows Mon–Fri 11–4, weekends 2–4 🚊 Tram 7 ♿ Good 💶 Moderate

KINDER KOEK KAFÉ
A children's restaurant where children between five and twelve can cook, then serve or eat at mini-tables.
➕ H5 ✉ Oudeijds Achterburgwal 193 ☎ 6253257 🕐 Sat cooking 3:30–6, dinner 6–8 (age 8 plus); Sun cooking 2:30–5, high tea 5–6 (age 5 plus). Mon–Fri private birthday parties only 🚇 Nieuwmarkt 💶 Very cheap

KINDERTHEATER ELLEBOOG
Learn tightrope-walking, juggling and other circus skills at the Elleboog Circus.
➕ G5 ✉ Passeerdersgracht 32 ☎ 6269370 🕐 Alternate weekends, Sat 1:30–5, Sun 10:30–4 🚊 Tram 7, 10 ♿ Good 💶 Moderate

MADAME TUSSAUD SCENERAMA
Meet wax models of Rembrandt, Pavarotti, Schwarzenegger and other characters from the 17th century to the present day, and an amazing 5m giant clothed in windmills and tulips.
➕ H5 ✉ Dam 20 ☎ 6229239 🕐 Sep–Jun, 10–5:30; Jul–Aug, 9:30–7:30 🚊 Tram 4, 9, 14, 16, 24, 25 ♿ Good 💶 Very expensive

NINT TECHNOLOGIE MUSEUM
Everyone enjoys this impressive hands-on museum of modern technology.
➕ J7 ✉ Tolstraat 129 ☎ 5708111 🕐 Mon–Fri 10–5, weekends 12–5 🍴 Café 🚊 Tram 4 ♿ Very good 💶 Moderate

Out of town

Ask the VVV for excursion details to Volendam, where villagers still wear traditional costumes; the windmill village of Zaanse Schans; to Zuiderzee, for the reconstructed fishing village of Enkhuizen, or to one of Holland's many theme parks, such as the enchanted forest of De Efteling at Kaatsheuvel or the Duinrell water park at Wassenaar, near the Hague.

Punch & Judy

Over the summer there are free Punch and Judy performances on Wed 1–5 in Dam Square.

Owl statue at the zoo

WINDMILLS

Amsterdam's most central windmill has been converted into a bar

D'ADMIRAAL
Built in 1792 to grind chalk but now unused.
➕ K1 ✉ Noordhollandsch Kanaaldijk, near Jan Thoméepad
🚌 Bus 34, 37, 39, 242

DE BLOEM
This old corn mill, built in 1768, resembles a giant pepperpot.
➕ F3 ✉ Haarlemmerweg, near Nieuwpoortkade 🚌 Bus 18

DE GOOIER (FUNENMOLEN)
Amsterdam's most central mill (1725) was the first corn mill in Holland to use the streamlined sails that became ubiquitous. Built on a brick base, with an octagonal body and a thatched wooden frame, it has been converted into a bar (▶ 81), but its massive sails still occasionally creak into action.
➕ K5 ✉ Funenkade 🚌 Tram 6, 10; Bus 22, 28

DE RIEKER
The finest windmill in Amsterdam was built in 1636 to drain the Rieker polder, and is situated at the southern tip of the Amstel Park. This was one of Rembrandt's favourite painting locations – there is a small statue near by in his memory. The windmill has been beautifully preserved and is now a private home.
➕ Off map to south ✉ Amsteldijk, near De Borcht 🚌 Bus 148

1100 ROE
This old smock mill, shaped like a peasant's smock, was once one of a '*gang*' of watermills used to drain the polders. It stands 1,100 roes from the city's outer canal – the word *roe* means both the flat part of a sail which had to be set or reefed according to wind strength, and a unit of measurement (about 28cm) used to calculate the distance from the city centre.
➕ A5 ✉ Herman Bonpad, Sportpark Ookmeer 🚌 Bus 19, 23

1200 ROE
This early 17th-century post mill, with its impressive platform and revolving cap, was built to help drain the polders.
➕ B3 ✉ Haarlemmerweg, near Willem Molengraaffstraat
🚌 Bus 85

National Windmill Day
Windmills have been a feature of the Dutch landscape since the 13th century. Much of the Netherlands lies below sea level, and windmills were used to drain the land and extend the shoreline, creating the fertile farmland called *polder*. Some 950 survive, and on National Windmill Day (the second Saturday in May), many turn their sails and are open to the public.

AMSTERDAM
where to...

DUTCH RESTAURANTS

Going Dutch

Numerous restaurants in the city provide a taste of authentic Dutch cuisine. The most delicious dishes include thick split-pea soup (*erwtensoep*), meaty stews (*stamppot*), smoked eel (*gerookt paling*), raw herring (*haring*), sweet and savoury pancakes (*pannekoeken*), waffles (*stroopwafels*), and cheeses. Look out for the special 'Neerlands Dis' sign (a red, white and blue soup tureen), which indicates restaurants commended for excellent value and high quality cuisine.

DE BLAUWE HOLLANDER (£)

Generous portions of wholesome Dutch fare are served here in a lively bistro atmosphere.

✚ G6 ✉ Leidsekruisstraat 28
☎ 6233014 🕐 Dinner only
🚋 Tram 1, 2, 5, 6, 7, 10

DE BLAUWE PARADE (££)

Since 1870, this famous restaurant has sold nearly six million numbered Dutch steaks. Every thousandth one comes with a free bottle of house wine.

✚ H5 ✉ Nieuwezijds Voorburgwal 178 ✉ 6240047
🚋 Tram 1, 2, 5, 13, 17

DORRIUS (£££)

Classic Dutch cuisine. Try the eel and salted cod traditional delicacies, or the cheese soufflé.

✚ H4 ✉ Nieuwe Voorburgwal 5 ☎ 4202224 🚋 Tram 1, 2, 5, 13, 17

DE GEUS (£)

Dutch pea soup, herring in *jenever* (gin), and warm cheesecake are some of the mouthwatering dishes served here.

✚ G6 ✉ Korte Leidsedwarsstraat 71
☎ 6271808 🚋 Tram 1, 2, 5, 6, 7, 10

HAESJE CLAES (££)

Dutch cuisine at its best, served in a warren of small, panelled dining rooms. The building dates from the 16th century, and the restaurant rooms are authentically furnished. Reservations necessary.

✚ G5 ✉ 273–275 Spui
☎ 6249998 🚋 Tram 1, 2, 5

HOLLAND'S GLORIE (££)

Traditional cuisine in a family atmosphere. Delft tiles and stained glass enhance the setting.

✚ H6 ✉ Kerkstraat 220–222
☎ 6244764 🕐 Dinner only
🚋 Tram 16, 24, 25

DE KEUKEN VAN 1870 (£)

Originally a soup kitchen, this old-fashioned establishment serves huge platefuls of cheap, no-frills food at communal tables.

✚ H4 ✉ Spuistraat 4
☎ 6248963 🕐 Mon–Fri 12:30–8; weekends 4–9
🚋 Tram 1, 2, 5, 13, 17

DE MOLEN 'DE DIKKERT' (£££)

Dine in a majestic old windmill on the outskirts of Amsterdam. Traditional Dutch cuisine.

✚ Off map to south
✉ Amsterdamseweg 104
☎ 6411378 🕐 Closed Sun
🚌 Bus 175

DE ROODE LEEUW (££)

Come to the 'Red Lion' for a taste of local home cooking. The stews and sauerkraut dishes are particularly good value.

✚ H5 ✉ Damrak 93–94
☎ 5550666 🕐 10AM–midnight, last orders 8PM
🚋 Tram 4, 9, 16, 24, 25

D'VIJFF VLIEGHEN (£££)

The ancient 'Five Flies' restaurant in five 17th-century houses boasts an impressive menu of 'new Dutch' cuisine.

✚ G5 ✉ 294–302 Spuistraat
☎ 6248369 🕐 Dinner only
🚋 Tram 1, 2, 5

GOURMET RESTAURANTS

BEDDINGTON'S (£££)

Imaginative French and Far Eastern cuisine in English chef Jean Beddington's strikingly modern restaurant.

G7 ✉ Roelof Hartstraat 6–8 ☎ 6765201 🕐 Closed Sun and lunch Mon 🚋 Tram 3, 5, 12, 24

CAFÉ ROUX (££)

Fine French cuisine in an elegant art nouveau setting.

H5 ✉ Oude Zijds Voorburgwal 197 ☎ 5553560 🚋 Nieuwmarkt

LE CIEL BLEU (£££)

The height of elegant dining – an award-winning French restaurant on the Okura Hotel's 23rd floor.

H7 ✉ Ferdinand Bolstraat 333 ☎ 6787111 🕐 Dinner only 🚋 Tram 12, 25

DE GOUDEN REAEL (££)

An elegant French restaurant in a 17th-century quayside building with a waterside terrace – perfect for a romantic evening.

H3 ✉ Zandhoek 14, Westerdok ☎ 6233883 🚌 Bus 28, Tram 3

LA RIVE (£££)

A leading restaurant in Amsterdam's most expensive hotel. Chef Robert Kranenborg is considered by many to be Holland's finest.

J6 ✉ Amstel Hotel, Professor Tulpplein 1 ☎ 6226060 🚇 Weesperplein

DE SILVEREN SPIEGEL (£££)

An exquisite *haute cuisine* menu, complemented by one of the city's best wine lists. Fish is a speciality in this immaculately restored 1614 house.

H4 ✉ Kattengatt 4–6 ☎ 6246589 🕐 Dinner only. Closed Sun except for parties which have booked 🚋 Tram 1, 2, 5, 13, 17

L'SWARTE SCHAEP (££)

The 'Black Sheep' is noted for its rustic atmosphere, excellent wines and blend of classic, nouvelle and post-modern cuisine.

G6 ✉ Korte Leidsedwarsstraat 24 ☎ 6223021 🚋 Tram 1, 2, 5, 6, 7, 10

TOUT COURT (£££)

This arty restaurant is a place to see and be seen in.

G5 ✉ Runstraat 13 ☎ 6258637 🕐 Mon–Fri noon–11.30, Sat & Sun 5PM–11.30PM 🚋 Tram 1, 2, 5

DE TRECHTER (££)

Book well in advance for this tiny, exclusive nouvelle cuisine restaurant.

G7 ✉ Hobbemakade 63 ☎ 6711263 🕐 Closed Sun and Mon 🚋 Tram 3, 12, 24

HET TUYNHUIS (££)

This converted coach house and garden provide the perfect setting for a special occasion. Sophisticated French, Portuguese and Dutch cuisine.

H5 ✉ Reguliersdwarsstraat 28 ☎ 6276603 🕐 Closed Sat & Sun lunch 🚋 Tram 4, 9, 14, 16, 24, 25

Opening times and prices

The restaurants listed on pages 62–68 are all open for lunch and dinner daily unless otherwise stated. They are divided into three price categories. For a main dish, expect to pay:

£££   over f50

££   up to f50

£   up to f25

Tipping

Most restaurants display menus in their windows, giving the price of individual dishes including BTW (purchase tax) and a 15 per cent service charge. Nevertheless, most Amsterdammers round up a small bill to the largest whole guilder and larger ones to the nearest f5. This tip should be left as change rather than included on a credit-card payment.

INDONESIAN RESTAURANTS

A hearty meal

First-timers to an Indonesian restaurant should order a *rijsttafel*, which includes rice and a complete range of other dishes: *ayam* (chicken), *ikam* (fish), *telor* (egg) and *rendang* (beef), *krupuk* (shrimp crackers), shredded coconut, and sweet-and-sour vegetables. The *rijsttafel* ('rice table') originally meant the long list of ingredients required to prepare such a feast. It originated in early colonial days among hungry Dutch planters who, not satisfied by the basic Indonesian meal of rice and vegetables accompanied by meat or fish, continually added other dishes. Thus the Rijsttafel was born.

ANEKA RASA (££)
This airy modern restaurant offers numerous vegetarian dishes including an all-vegetarian *rijsttafel*.
✚ H5 ✉ Warmoesstraat 25–29 ☎ 6261560 ☐ Centraal Station

INDRAPURA (££)
A popular colonial-style restaurant. Tell the waiter how hot and spicy you want your dishes to be.
✚ H5 ✉ Rembrandtplein 42 ☎ 6237329 ☻ Dinner only ☐ Tram 4, 9, 14

JAYAKARTA (££)
Right at the heart of one of Amsterdam's liveliest nightlife districts and ideal for a late-evening meal.
✚ H5 ✉ Rembrandtplein 16 ☎ 6255569 ☐ Tram 4, 9 14, 16, 24, 25

KANTJIL EN DE TIJGER (££)
A successful combination of modern decor and spicy, imaginative cuisine. Try the delicious *Masi Rames*, a mini-*rijsttafel* on one plate.
✚ G5 ✉ Spuistraat 291 ☎ 6200994 ☻ Dinner only ☐ Tram 1, 2, 5

ORIENT (££)
This dark, opulent restaurant offers more than 20 different sorts of *rijsttafel*, and an extensive buffet on Wednesdays.
✚ G6 ✉ van Baerlestraat 21 ☎ 6734958 ☻ Dinner only ☐ Tram 2, 3, 5, 12

SAHID JAYA (££)
The shady courtyard garden provides the perfect setting for a meal during summer.
✚ H5 ✉ Reguliersdwarsstraat 26 ☎ 6263727 ☐ Tram 16, 24, 25

SAMA SEBO (££)
This Balinese-style restaurant is an old favourite with Amsterdammers and local Indonesians.
✚ G6 ✉ P C Hooftstraat 27 ☎ 6628146 ☻ Closed Sun ☐ Tram 2, 5

SPECIAAL (££)
One of the most popular Indonesian restaurants in town, hidden in a back street in the Jordaan. The *rijsttafel* is a sight to behold.
✚ G4 ✉ Nieuwe Leliestraat 142 ☎ 6249706 ☻ Dinner only ☐ Tram 10, 13, 14, 17

SUKASARI (£)
Colourful batik tablecloths and closely packed tables provide a cheerful atmosphere. The generous portions are good value.
✚ H5 ✉ Damstraat 26 ☎ 6240092 ☻ Mon–Sat noon–9PM ☐ Tram 4, 9, 16, 24, 25

TEMPO DOELO (££)
One of Amsterdam's best Indonesian restaurants, famous for its western-style interior, exotic flower arrangements and some of the hottest dishes in town
✚ H6 ✉ Utrechtsestraat 75 ☎ 6256718 ☻ Dinner only ☐ Tram 4

VEGETARIAN & FISH RESTAURANTS

BODEGA 'KEYSER' (££)

An Amsterdam institution next door to the Concertgebouw, specialising in fish and traditional Dutch dishes.

✚ G6 ✉ Van Baerlestraat 96
☎ 6711441 ◷ 9AM–midnight.
Closed Sun 🚋 Tram 2, 3, 5, 12

BOLHOED (£)

A trendy restaurant on the edge of the Jordaan, with a wide choice of vegetarian pâtés, salads and hearty vegan dishes.

✚ G4 ✉ Prinsengracht 60
☎ 6261803 🚋 Tram 13, 14, 17

GOLDEN TEMPLE (£)

An imaginative menu of Indian, Mexican and Middle Eastern dishes.

✚ H6 ✉ Utrechtsestraat 126
☎ 6268560 ◷ Dinner only
🚋 Tram 4

HEMELSE MODDER (££)

Sophisticated main courses and delicious desserts including 'Heavenly Mud', the chocolate mousse from which the restaurant takes its name. Customers are admitted only until 10PM, but you can linger much later over your meal if you want.

✚ H5 ✉ Oude Waal 9
☎ 243203 ◷ Dinner only
6–10 (last admission)
Ⓜ Nieuwmarkt

KLAVIERKONING (££)

A fish and vegetarian restaurant with good wines.

✚ H5 ✉ Koniingsstraat 29
☎ 6261085 ◷ Dinner only.
Closed Mon Ⓜ Nieuwmarkt

DE OESTERBAR (££)

The seasonal delights of this elegant fish restaurant on Leidseplein include herring in May, mussels in June and delicate Zeeland oysters throughout the summer.

✚ G6 ✉ Leidseplein 10
☎ 6232988 🚋 Tram 1, 2, 5, 6, 7, 10

LE PECHEUR (£££)

A smart, bistro-style fish restaurant with a secluded terrace garden. Outstanding fresh oysters, caviar, sashimi and lobster.

✚ H5 ✉ Reguliersdwarsstraat 32 ☎ 6243121 ◷ Closed Sat lunch and all day Sun 🚋 Tram 1, 2, 5

SHIZEN (££)

Enjoy delectable Japanese fish and organic vegetable dishes whilst sitting on tatami mats.

✚ H6 ✉ Kerkstraat 148
☎ 6228627 ◷ Closed Mon
🚋 Tram 16, 24, 25

SISTERS DINER (£)

Generous portions of tempting dishes in a casual, friendly atmosphere.

✚ H5 ✉ Nes 102
☎ 6263970 ◷ Dinner only
🚋 Tram 4, 9, 14, 16, 24, 25

VISRESTAURANT 'JULIA' (££)

Julia's famous fish platter (with 10 kinds of fish) draws people from all over the region.

✚ Off map to south
✉ Amstelveenseweg 160
☎ 6795394 ◷ Dinner only
🚌 Bus 146, 147, 170, 171, 172

Vegetarian food

Although the Dutch are primarily a meat-eating race, Amsterdam caters well for vegetarians, with specialist vegetarian eating places to suit all tastes and budgets. Many other restaurants also offer vegetarian dishes on the menu, especially the numerous pizzerias and oriental restaurants dotted around town.

INTERNATIONAL RESTAURANTS

ASIAN CARIBBEAN EXPERIENCE (£)

Choose from over 100 dishes from all over Asia and the Caribbean.

🚻 H5   ✉ Warmoesstraat 170   ☎ 6271545   🕐 Dinner only   🚋 Tram 4, 9, 16, 24, 25

BRASSERIE RENTRÉE (££)

A truly international menu served in a romantic, candlelit setting.

🚻 H4   ✉ Zeedijk 29   ☎ 6389340   🕐 Daily, dinner only 5:30–11 (last admission)   🚉 Centraal Station

CAFÉ PACIFICO (££)

The most authentic Mexican bodega in town. Especially crowded on *margarita* nights (Tue)

🚻 H4   ✉ Warmoesstraat 31   ☎ 6242911   🕐 Dinner only. Closed Mon   🚉 Centraal Station

CHEZ GEORGES (££)

Fine Belgian cuisine in a classical, candlelit restaurant.

🚻 G4   ✉ Herenstraat 3   ☎ 6263332   🕐 Closed Sat lunch, all Sun & Wed   🚋 Tram 1, 2, 5, 13, 17

DYNASTY (£££)

A sophisticated, sumptuously decorated garden restaurant serving fine Southeast Asian cuisine.

🚻 H5   ✉ Reguliersdwarsstraat 30   ☎ 6268400   🕐 Dinner only. Closed Tue   🚋 Tram 16, 24, 25

EL RANCHO ARGENTINIAN GRILL (££)

Sizzling steaks and spare ribs in a jolly ranch-like atmosphere.

🚻 H5   ✉ Spui 3   ☎ 6256764   🕐 11AM–midnight   🚋 Tram 4, 9, 14, 16, 24, 25

DE FLES BISTRO (££)

Gather round large wooden tables with the locals in this cosy cellar on the elegant Prinsengracht canal.

🚻 H6   ✉ Prinsengracht 955   ☎ 6249644   🕐 Dinner only   🚋 Tram 16, 24, 25

FROMAGERIE CRIGNON CULINAIR (£)

This rustic restaurant boasts eight different types of cheese fondu.

🚻 H5   ✉ Gravenstraat 28   ☎ 6246428   🕐 6AM–9.30PM. Closed Sun, Mon   🚋 Tram 4, 9, 16, 24, 25

GAUGUIN (££)

The restaurant's slogan 'Where East meets West' reflects the exotic mix of dishes and the colourful South Seas-style interior design.

🚻 G6   ✉ Leidsekade 110   ☎ 6221526   🕐 Dinner only. Closed Mon, Tue   🚋 Tram 1, 2, 5, 6, 7, 10

MEMORIES OF INDIA (££)

Tandoori, Moghlai, and vegetarian cuisine in elegant surroundings.

🚻 H5   ✉ Reguliersdwarsstraat 88   ☎ 6235710   🕐 Dinner only   🚋 Tram 4, 9, 14

PAKISTAN (££)

Holland's top Pakistani restaurant. The menu ranges from traditional, village dishes to highly spiced specialities.

🚻 F5   ✉ De Clercqstraat 65   ☎ 6181120   🕐 Dinner only   🚋 Tram 3, 12, 13, 14

Surinamese cuisine

Explore the narrow streets of the multi-racial district around Albert Cuypstraat, and you will soon realise how easy it is to eat your way around the world in Amsterdam. The many Surinamese restaurants here serve a delicious blend of African, Chinese and Indian cuisine. Specialities include *bojo* (cassava and coconut quiche) and *pitjil* (baked vegetables with peanut sauce). Try them at Marowijne (✉ Albert Cuypstraat 68–70), or Wan Pipel (✉ Albert Cuypstraat 140).

PASTA E BASTA (££)

Pasta in chic surroundings, accompanied by opera classics.

➕ G6 ✉ Nieuwe Speigelstraat 8 ☎ 4222229 🚊 Tram 16, 24, 25

PIER 10 (££)

This former shipping office offers an innovative menu with an emphasis on fish, and an unusual ship-side location on the River IJ. It is set right on Pier 10 – one of the series of jetties where ships dock.

➕ H4 ✉ De Ruijterkade, Pier 10 ☎ 6248276 🕐 Dinner only 🚊 Tram 1, 2, 4, 5, 9, 13, 16, 17, 24, 25

ROSE'S CANTINA (££)

Excellent value Tex-Mex meals in lively, sociable surroundings. Probably Amsterdam's most crowded restaurant.

➕ H5 ✉ Reguliersdwarsstraat 38 ☎ 6259797 🚊 Tram 16, 24, 25

RUM RUNNERS (££)

The giant palms, caged parrots, live music, spicy stews and wicked cocktails give this Caribbean-style restaurant a distinctly tropical feel.

➕ G4 ✉ Prinsengracht 277 ☎ 6274079 🕐 Mon–Fri from 4PM. Weekends from 2PM 🚊 Tram 13, 14, 17

SAUDADE (££)

A Portuguese restaurant with dockside terrace, at the heart of the fashionable Entrepotdok district.

➕ L5 ✉ Entrepotdok 36 ☎ 6254845 🚊 Bus 22

SUKHOTHAI (££)

Exotic, spicy Thai dishes in amospheric bamboo and palm surroundings. Try their speciality – Nua Pad Prik Bai Kra Pauw – if you can pronounce it!

➕ H7 ✉ Ceinturbaan 147 ☎ 6718086 🕐 Dinner only Closed Tue 🚊 Tram 3

TANGO (££)

Small, candlelit restaurant on the edge of the Red Light District. Try the huge, juicy steaks, grilled on an open fire and served with delicious corn-based humitas. Not for vegetarians!

➕ H4 ✉ Warmoesstraat 49 ☎ 6272467 🕐 Dinner only 🚊 Tram 4, 9, 16, 24, 25

TEPPANYAKI NIPPON (££)

One of Holland's most elegant and exclusive Japanese grill-restaurants, with virtuoso service.

➕ H5 ✉ Reguliersdwarsstraat 18–20 ☎ 6208787 🕐 Dinner only 🚊 Tram 16, 24, 25

TOSCANINI (££)

Book well in advance for the best Italian food in town.

➕ G4 ✉ Lindengracht 75 ☎ 6232813 🕐 Dinner only. Closed Tue 🚊 Tram 3

LE ZINC... ET LES DAMES (££)

Home-style French cuisine in a converted canalside warehouse. The *tarte tatin* is divine.

➕ H6 ✉ Prinsengracht 999 ☎ 6229044 🕐 Dinner only. Closed Sun & Mon 🚊 Tram 4

A taste of china

Amsterdam is home to the largest Chinese community in Europe and as a result boasts numerous superb Chinese eateries. One of the most popular is Treasure (✉ Nieuwezijds Voorburgwal 115–17), with specialities from Beijing, Shanghai and Canton provinces. For something cheap but good, try Si-chuan (✉ Lange Niezel 24), with its unusual Tibetan and Szechuan dishes. The Sea Palace (✉ Osterdokskade 8), advertises itself as Europe's first floating restaurant. It is modelled on a Chinese pagoda-style palace and is the next best thing to its prototype, Hong Kong's famous *Jumbo* restaurant.

SNACKS & *EETCAFÉS*

A bite to 'eet'

For cheap but substantial snacks, try an *eetcafé* for filling homemade fare (soup, sandwiches and omelettes) but remember that the kitchens close around 9PM. Market stalls often serve local delicacies, and most bars offer *borrelhapjes* ('mouthfuls with a glass') – usually olives, chunks of cheese or *borrelnoten* (nuts with a savoury coating). For a really quick snack, the many *Febo* food dispensers about town are excellent: simply put your money in and your snack comes out hot.

CAFÉ DANTZIG (£)
Giant, crusty baguettes with delicious fillings make a perfect lunch on the terrace beside the Amstel river.
➕ H5 ✉ Zwanenburgwal 15
☎ 6209039 ⏰ 10AM–1AM
🚇 Waterlooplein

CAFÉ KORT (££)
A delightfully located café-cum-restaurant on the corner of Prinsengracht and Reguliersgracht, with a charming shady terrace beside the canals.
➕ H6 ✉ Amstelfeld 12
☎ 6261199 🚊 Tram 4

KAAS-WIJNHUIS (£)
Wines, cheeses, cold cuts and pâtés in a charming delicatessen-cum-*eetcafé*.
➕ H4 ✉ Wamoesstraat 16
☎ 6230878 ⏰ Mon–Sat 9–6, Sun noon–6 🚇 Centraal Station

LATE NIGHT BAGELS (£)
As the name suggests, a late-night snack store, in a street of trendy bars and clubs. Also open during the day.
➕ H5 ✉ Reguliersdwarsstraat 53 ☎ 4202406 ⏰ 10AM–3AM (Fri & Sat 4AM) 🚊 Tram 4, 9, 14, 16, 24, 25

LUNCHROOM DIALOGUE (£)
Enjoy the sandwiches and sticky cakes in a warehouse cellar, away from the crowds at Anne Frankhuis next door.
➕ G4 ✉ Prinsengracht 261a
☎ 6239991 ⏰ Daily 10–5
🚊 Tram 13, 14, 17

MORITA-YA (£)
This tiny Japanese snack-bar is a must for sushi fans.
➕ H4 ✉ Zeedijk 18
☎ 6380756 ⏰ Dinner only, closed Wed 🚇 Centraal Station

PANCAKE BAKERY (£)
The best pancakes in town, cooked on an old Dutch griddle.
➕ G5 ✉ Prinsengracht 191
☎ 6251333 🚊 Tram 13, 14, 17

LA PLACE (£)
A self-service 'indoor market' restaurant. Choose your dish at one of the stands, watch it being cooked, then eat at one of the tables.
➕ H5 ✉ Rokin 164
☎ 6202364 ⏰ 9AM–9PM except Thu 9AM–10PM, Sun noon–9PM 🚊 Tram 4, 9, 14, 16, 24, 25

SMALL TALK (££)
Near the Museumplein, this *eetcafé* is ideal for soups and snacks between gallery visits.
➕ G6 ✉ Van Baerlestraat 52
☎ 6714864 🚊 Tram 2, 3, 5, 12

TAPAS CATALA (£)
Enjoy a quick bite or a meal of tempting tapas dishes.
➕ G5 ✉ Spuistraat 299
☎ 6231141 ⏰ Dinner only. Closed Tue 🚊 Tram 1, 2, 5

VAN DOBBEN (£)
A renowned sandwich shop. Try a meat croquette roll, which Van Dobben makes himself from a 50-year-old recipe.
➕ H5 ✉ Korte Reguliersdwarsstraat 5–9
☎ 6244200 ⏰ Mon–Thu 9:30AM–1PM, Fri–Sat 9:30AM–2PM, Sun 11:30AM–8PM 🚊 Tram 4, 9, 14

CAFÉS & TEA SHOPS

BACKSTAGE (£)

A wacky, psychedelic café run by the eccentric 'Christmas Twins' comic actors.

✚ H6 ✉ Utrechtsedwarsstraat 67 ☎ 6223638 ⏰ Daily 10–6 🚋 Tram 4

BOLLEBEER (£)

A café geared to children. Teddy bears outnumber the seats.

✚ H5 ✉ Kloveniersburgwal 38 ☎ 6243102 ⏰ Mon–Sat 10–8. Closed Sun 🚋 Tram 4, 9, 14, 16, 24, 25

CAFÉ AMERICAIN (£)

Artists and writers have frequented this grandiose art deco café since the turn of the century.

✚ G6 ✉ Leidseplein 28 ☎ 6245322 ⏰ 7AM–1AM 🚋 Tram 1, 2, 5, 6, 7, 10

CAFÉ VERTIGO (££)

Theme menus, reflecting what is on at the adjacent Film Museum.

✚ G6 ✉ Vondelpark 3 ☎ 6123021 🚋 Tram 1, 6

CAFFÉ ESPRIT

This designer café, all glass and aluminium, is run by the clothing chain next door, and, not surprisingly, is a popular coffee stop for shoppers.

✚ H5 ✉ Spui 10a ☎ 6221967 ⏰ Mon–Sat 10–6 (Thu until 10PM), Sun noon–6 🚋 Tram 1, 2, 4, 5, 9, 14, 16, 24, 25

METZ (£)

The views from the top floor café of this department store (▶71) are among the finest in the city.

✚ G5 ✉ Keizersgracht 455 ☎ 6248810 🚋 Tram 1, 2, 5

NIEUWE KAFÉ (£)

The café's crowded terrace on Dam Square provides a captive audience for buskers, and an ideal venue for people-watching.

✚ H5 ✉ Eggertstraat 8 ☎ 6272830 ⏰ 8:30–6 🚋 Tram 4, 9, 14, 16, 24, 25

POMPADOUR (£)

The finest chocolatier in town also doubles up as a sumptuous tearoom.

✚ G5 ✉ Huidenstraat 12 ☎ 6239554 ⏰ Mon 1–6, Tue–Sat 9–6 🚋 Tram 1, 2, 5

LA RUCHE (£)

Treat yourself to coffee with waffles piled high with fresh strawberries and cream in the café of De Bijenkorf department store (▶72), overlooking Dam.

✚ H5 ✉ 1 Dam ☎ 6218080 ⏰ Daily 9:30–6, except Thu 9:30–9, Sat noon–5 🚋 Tram 4, 9, 14, 16, 24, 25

TUINHOF (££)

This stylish restaurant serves afternoon tea every day from 3pm. Choose from scones, crumpets and a mouthwatering array of cakes.

✚ H4 ✉ Zeedijk 23 ⏰ Centraal Station

WINKEL (£)

A popular locals' café in the midst of the Noordermarkt (▶53). Great for people-watching!

✚ G4 ✉ Noodermarkt 43 ☎ 6230223 ⏰ Closed evenings 🚋 Trams 3, 10

Coffee shops

Be warned! The expression 'coffee shop' is open to misinterpretation in Amsterdam, as it usually refers to the 'smoking' coffee shops where youngsters hang out, high on hash. Although strictly speaking illegal, the sale and use of soft drugs is tolerated by the authorities. 'Smoking' coffee shops are easily recognisable by their psychedelic decor, marijuana plants and mellowed people staring into space. If you are offered 'space cake' instead of fruit cake, you know you are in the wrong kind of coffee shop!

SHOPPING AREAS

Opening hours

Most shops are open Tuesday to Saturday from 9AM or 10AM until 6PM, and on Mondays from 1PM until 6PM, with late-night shopping on Thursdays until 9PM. Many shops open noon–5PM on Sundays too. Cash is the most popular method of payment, although credit cards and Eurocheques are accepted at most department stores and larger shops. Guard your money closely, as pickpockets abound in the main shopping streets.

Amsterdam has over 10,000 shops and department stores, although it does not compare with Paris or London for *haute couture* and European chic. But the large number of unusual specialist stores, secondhand shops and colourful markets dotted around the canals make shopping here a real pleasure. Interesting souvenirs and gifts to take home are easy to find, whatever your budget.

ART & ANTIQUES

Antique shops are concentrated in the *Spiegelkwartier* near the Museumplein, along and around Nieuwe Spiegelstraat, and along the Rokin. Countless commercial galleries are scattered throughout the city rather than confined to one specific area, although many can be found along the main canals.

BOOKSHOPS

Most of the city's bookshops are located around the university district (off the Spui) and in Leidsestraat. You will also find several specialist antique bookstores on Nieuwezijds Voorburgwal, and there is an indoor antiquarian book market at Oudemanhuispoort.

FASHION

The three main shopping thoroughfares – Kalverstraat, Nieuwendijk and Leidsestraat – are lined with international chain stores and mainstream outlets for clothing and accessories. To the south, P C Hooftstraat, van Baerlestraat and Beethovenstraat play host to designer stores. For alternative, more adventurous garb, head to the Jordaan.

SECONDHAND

Take time to explore the secondhand stores of the Jordaan for a bargain, or sift your way through local street markets, including the city's largest and wackiest fleamarket at Waterlooplein.

SHOPPING CENTRES (MALLS)

There are four main shopping centres: chic Magna Plaza near Dam Square; De Amsterdamse Poort, reached by metro at Amsterdam Zuid-Oost; Winkelcentrum Boven't IJ, reached by ferry across the IJ, and Schiphol Plaza at the airport, open from 7AM until 10PM daily and ideal for last minute present-shopping.

DUTCH SOUVENIRS & GIFTS

AMSTERDAM SMALLEST GALLERY

An original, fun painting of the city bought here will remind you of your stay in Amsterdam.

🞢 G4 ✉ Westermarkt 60
☎ 6223756 🚋 Tram 13, 14, 17

BONEBAKKER

Dazzling displays of gold and silverware at Holland's royal jewellers. An enjoyable place for a bit of window-shopping, even if you can't afford to buy.

🞢 H5 ✉ Rokin 86–90
☎ 6232294 🚋 Tram 4, 9, 14, 16, 24, 25

DAM SQUARE SOUVENIRS

Centrally placed souvenir shop with an impressive choice of clogs, furnishings, pottery and T-shirts.

🞢 H5 ✉ Dam 17
☎ 6203432 🚋 Tram 4, 9, 14, 16, 24, 25

FOCKE & MELTZER

A superior gift shop, with a broad choice of Dutch glassware, silver and porcelain.

🞢 G6 ✉ P C Hooftstraat 65
☎ 6642311 🚋 Tram 2, 3, 5, 12

HEINEN HANDPAINTED DELFTWARE

Delightful Delftware plates, tulip vases and Christmas decorations are the speciality in this tiny store.

🞢 G4 ✉ Prinsengracht 440
☎ 6278299 🚋 Tram 1, 2, 5, 13, 17

HOLLAND GALLERY DE MUNT

Miniature ceramic canal houses, dolls in traditional costume, ornately decorated wooden boxes, and trays.

🞢 H5 ✉ Muntplein 12
☎ 6232271 🚋 Tram 4, 9, 14, 16, 24, 25

HET KANTENHUIS

Exquisite handmade Dutch lace.

🞢 H5 ✉ Kalverstraat 124
☎ 6248618 🚋 Tram 4, 9, 14, 16, 24, 25

DE KLOMPENBOER

This authentic clog factory offers the city's largest selection of hand-crafted footwear, amidst roaming cats and chickens.

🞢 H4 ✉ Nieuwezijds Voorburgwal 20 ☎ 6230632
🚋 Tram 1, 2, 5, 13, 17

METZ & CO

An emporium of expensive gifts and designer furniture. One of the city's most stylish department stores, and it also has a café on the top floor (▶ 69).

🞢 G5 ✉ Keizersgracht 455
☎ 6248810 🚋 Tram 1, 2, 5

DE TUIN

The Bloemenmarkt (flower market) (▶ 38) is the cheapest place to buy bulbs and this stall has the widest selection.

🞢 H5 ✉ Bloemenmarkt (opposite Singel 502)
☎ 6254571 🚋 Tram 4, 9, 14, 16, 24, 25

Spoilt for Choice

Some typically Dutch gifts:

Bulbs

Made-to-measure clogs

Bottle of *jenever* (Dutch gin)

Edam or Gouda cheese

Diamonds

Leerdam crystal

Makkum pottery

Delftware –if you want the real thing look for De Porcelyne Fles (see panel ▶ 21)

An old print or map of the city

Trendy clothing

FOOD, DRINK & DEPARTMENT STORES

Say cheese!

Think Dutch cheese and the distinctive red *Edammer* and *Goudse* (from Gouda) spring to mind. They can be young (*jong*) and mild, or more mature (*belegen*) and strong. Mild young cheeses such as *Leerdammer* and *Maaslander* deserve a tasting too. Others to try are *Friese Nagelkaas*, flavoured with cumin and cloves and *Gras Kaas* (grass cheese), sold in summer, which owes its especially creamy flavour to the fresh spring cow pastures.

DE BIERKONING
850 special beers and glasses from around the world.
✚ H5 ✉ Paleisstraat 125
☎ 6252336 🚊 Tram 1, 2, 5, 13, 14, 17

DE BIJENKORF
Amsterdam's busy main department store, the *Bijenkorf* ('Beehive') lives up to its name. See also La Ruche café (►69).
✚ H5 ✉ Dam 1
☎ 6218080 🚊 Tram 4, 9, 14, 16, 24, 25

EICHHOLTZ
Long-established delicatessen with Dutch, American and English specialities.
✚ G6 ✉ Leidsestraat 48
☎ 6220305 🚊 Tram 1, 2, 5

GEELS EN CO
Holland's oldest coffee roasting and tea trading company – a superb blend of heady aromas, helpful staff and traditional atmosphere.
✚ H4 ✉ Warmoesstraat 67
☎ 6240683 🚊 Tram 4, 9, 14, 16, 24, 25

HENDRIKSE PATISSERIE
Queen Beatrix buys her pastries here.
✚ F6 ✉ Overtoom 472
☎ 6180472 🚊 Tram 1, 6

H P DE VRENG & ZN
This celebrated wine-and-spirits establishment has been producing fine liqueurs and *jenevers* since 1852.
✚ H4 ✉ Nieuwendijk 75
☎ 6244581 🚊 Tram 1, 2, 5, 13, 17

J G BEUNE
Famous for chocolate *Amsterdammertjes* (the bollards lining the streets to prevent cars falling into the canals), and a mouth-watering array of cakes and bonbons.
✚ G4 ✉ Haarlemmerdijk 156–8 ☎ 6248356 🚊 Tram 1, 2, 5, 13, 17

MAISON DE LA BONNETERIE
A gracious department store, popular with wealthy ladies.
✚ H5 ✉ Rokin 150
☎ 6262162 🚊 Tram 4, 9, 14, 16, 24, 25

VITALS VITAMIN-ADVICE SHOP
Specialises exclusively in vitamins, minerals and other food supplements and offers customers a unique service: a computerised vitamin test!
✚ H4 ✉ Nieuwe Nieuwstraat 47 ☎ 6257298 🚊 Tram 1, 2, 5, 13, 17

DE WATERWINKEL
When you tire of beers, wines and Dutch gin, taste some of the hundred different mineral waters on offer here.
✚ G7 ✉ Roelof Hartstraat 10 ☎ 6755932 🚊 Tram 3, 12, 24

WOUT ARXHOEK
One of the best cheese shops with over 250 different varieties.
✚ H5 ✉ Damstraat 19
☎ 6229118 🚊 Tram 4, 9, 14, 16, 24, 25

ANTIQUES & BOOKSHOPS

AMSTERDAM ANTIQUES GALLERY

Six dealers under one roof, selling silverware, pewter, paintings, and Dutch tiles, amongst other items.

✚ G6 ✉ Nieuwe Spiegelstraat 34 ☎ 6253371 🚋 Tram 6, 7, 10

ATHENAEUM BOCKHANDEL

This long-established bookshop, in a striking art nouveau building, stocks international newspapers and specialises in social sciences, literature and the classics.

✚ G5 ✉ Spui 14–16 ☎ 6233933 🚋 Tram 1, 2, 5

BEN BIJLEFELD

Antique timepieces and nautical instruments in an old-world atmosphere.

✚ G6 ✉ Nieuwe Spiegelstraat 45a ☎ 6277774 🚋 Tram 6, 7, 10

EDUARD KRAMER

A treasure trove of old Dutch tiles, the earliest dating from 1580.

✚ G6
✉ Nieuwe Spiegelstraat 64 ☎ 6230832 🚋 Tram 6, 7, 10

EGIDIUS ANTIQUARISCHE BOEKHANDEL

A tiny shop packed with antique books on travel, photography and the arts.

✚ H5 ✉ Nieuwezijds Voorburgwal 334 ☎ 6243929 🚋 Tram 1, 2, 5

DE KINDER- BOEKWINKEL

A vast array of children's books, arranged according to age, with a good selection of titles available in English and German.

✚ G5 ✉ Rozengracht 34 ☎ 6224761 🚋 Tram 13, 14, 17

LAMBIEK

Lambiek claims to be the world's oldest comic shop.

✚ G6 ✉ Kerkstraat 78 ☎ 6267543 🚋 Tram 1, 2, 5

DE LOOIER KUNST- & ANTIEK-CENTRUM

A mecca for browsers and bargain-hunters. Hundreds of stalls in a covered antiques market, selling everything from quality collector's pieces to ageing junk.

✚ G5 ✉ Elandsgracht 109 ☎ 6249038 🚋 Tram 7, 10, 17

SCHELTEMA HOLKEMA VERMEULEN

The city's biggest bookstore, with a floor dedicated to multimedia.

✚ G5 ✉ Koningsplein 20 ☎ 5231411 🚋 Tram 1, 2, 5

DE SLEGTE

Amsterdam's largest secondhand bookshop is a good source of holiday-reading bargains, with plenty of English and German stock.

✚ H5 ✉ Kalverstraat 48–52 ☎ 6225933 🚋 Tram 4, 9, 14, 16, 24, 25

'T CACHOT

Secondhand thrillers and crime novels in the cell of what was once Holland's smallest police station.

✚ L9 ✉ Dorpsplein ☎ 6691795 🕐 Tue, Wed, Sat afternoons only 🚌 Bus 59, 60, 175

Going, going, gone!

Amsterdam's main auction houses are the international firms of Sotheby's (✉ Rokin 102 ☎ 5502200) and Christie's (✉ Cornelis Schuystraat 57 ☎ 5755255). Dutch counterpart, Veilinghuis (Auction House) de Nieuwe Zon, is at Overtoom 197 (☎ 6168586). All hold pre-sale viewings, interesting even if you have no intention to buy.

SPECIALIST SHOPS

Magna Plaza

Amsterdam's most luxurious shopping mall, the Magna Plaza, is housed in an imposing neo-Gothic building in Nieuwezijds Voorburgwal near Dam Square. Its four floors are filled with upmarket specialist shops, such as Pinokkio, for educational toys, Bjorn Borg, for sporty underwear, and Speeldozenwereld, for quaint musical boxes. There is a café on the top floor and a Virgin Megastore in the basement.

DE BEESTENWINKEL

A cuddly-toy shop for adults! Ideal for collectors and small gifts.

H5 ⊠ Staalstraat 11 ☎ 6231805 🚋 Tram 4, 9, 14, 16, 24, 25

CHRISTMAS WORLD

Sample the special atmosphere of Christmas in Holland all year round, amidst glittering displays of bobbles and bells.

H5 ⊠ Nieuwezijds Voorburgwal 137–9 ☎ 6227047 🚋 Tram 1, 2, 5, 13, 17

CONCERTO

New and used records and CDs to suit all tastes. The finest all-round selection in the city, especially good for jazz, classical music and hits from the '50s and '60s.

H6 ⊠ Utrechtsestraat 52–60 ☎ 6245467 🚋 Tram 4

CONDOMERIE HET GULDEN VLIES

The world's first specialised condom shop, located in a former squat.

H5 ⊠ Warmoesstraat 141 ☎ 6274174 🚋 Tram 4, 9, 14, 16, 24, 25

CONSCIOUS DREAMS

Anything's possible in Amsterdam....this shop specialises in 'magic mushrooms'!

H6 ⊠ Kerkstraat 117 ☎ 6266907 🚋 Tram 16, 24, 25

DEN HAAN & WAGENMAKERS

A patchwork-maker's paradise of traditional fabrics, tools and gadgets.

H4 ⊠ Nieuwezijds Voorburgwal 97–9 ☎ 6202525 🚋 Tram 1, 2, 5, 13, 17

FIFTIES-SIXTIES

A fine jumble of period pieces including toasters, teasmades, records, lamps and other working mementoes of this hip era.

G5 ⊠ Huidenstraat 13 ☎ 6232653 🚋 Tram 1, 2, 5

DE FIETSENMAKER

Recently voted the top bike shop in Amsterdam.

H5 ⊠ Nieuwe Hoogstraat 23–5 ☎ 6246137 🚇 Nieuwmarkt

HAIR POLICE

Come here for dreadlocks, extensions, braids or just a normal haircut.

H6 ⊠ Kerkstraat 113 ☎ 4205841 🚋 Tram 16, 24, 25

HEAD SHOP

The shop for marijuana memorabilia, ever since it opened in the '60s.

H5 ⊠ Kloveniersburgwal 39 ☎ 6249061 🚇 Nieuwmarkt

HEMP WORKS

Designer hemp store: jeans, jackets, shirts, shampoo and soap all made of hemp.

H4 ⊠ Nieuwendijk 13 ☎ 4211762 🚋 Tram 1, 2, 5, 13, 17

JACOB HOOIJ

This old-fashioned apothecary has been selling herbs, spices and homeopathic remedies since 1743.

H5 ⊠ Kloveniersburgwal 12 ☎ 6243041 🚇 Nieuwmarkt

KITSCH KITCHEN

Ghanaian metal furniture, Indian bead curtains, Mexican tablecloths, Chinese pots and pans – the whole world in one colourful kitchen!

✚ G5 ✉ Eerste Bloemdwarsstraat 21 ☎ 6228261 🚊 Tram 13, 14, 17

NORMAN AUTOMATICS

An Aladdin's cave overflowing with flashing neon advertisements, fruit machines, jukeboxes and even the odd traffic light.

✚ G5 ✉ Prinsengracht 292 ☎ 6380500 🚊 Tram 13, 14, 17

OUTRAS COISAS

Ancient and modern pots and gardening tools, reflecting the Dutch passion for plants.

✚ G4 ✉ Herenstraat 31 ☎ 6257281 🚊 Tram 1, 2, 5, 13, 14, 17

PARTY HOUSE

A cornucopia of paper decorations, dressing-up clothes, masks and practical jokes.

✚ G5 ✉ Rozengracht 93a–b ☎ 6247851 🚊 Tram 13, 14, 17

PAS-DESTOEL CHILDREN'S FURNITURE STORE

Children's dreams can come true at this colourful interior design store.

✚ G4 ✉ Westeerstraat 260 ☎ 4207542 🚊 Tram 13, 14, 17

P G C HAJENIUS

One of the world's finest tobacco shops, in elegant, art deco premises.

✚ H5 ✉ Rokin 92–96 ☎ 6237494 🚊 Tram 4, 9, 14, 16, 24, 25

RED EARTH

Pamper yourself with exotic body-care products made from natural ingredients and essential oils according to ancient Aboriginal recipes.

✚ G6 ✉ Leidsestraat 64–6 ☎ 6221620 🚊 Tram 1, 2, 5

SCALE TRAIN HOUSE

Take home a windmill or a canal barge as a souvenir just two of the many DIY kits on offer here, together with a vast stock of model railway components.

✚ F5 ✉ Bilderdijkstraat 94 ☎ 6122670 🚊 Tram 3, 12, 13, 14

DE SPEELMUIS

A splendid collection of handmade wooden toys and doll's house miniatures.

✚ G5 ✉ Elandsgracht 58 ☎ 6385342 🚊 Tram 7, 10, 17

SUPERCLUB

Listen to the latest chart toppers, surf the Internet or try a video game at this fun entertainment store.

✚ H4 ✉ Nieuwendijk 158 ☎ 6262342 🚊 Tram 4, 9, 14, 16, 24, 25

VLIEGERTUIG

There is always enough wind to fly a kite in Holland. This is one of several specialist kite shops in Amsterdam.

✚ G5 ✉ Gasthuismolensteeg 8 ☎ 6233450 🚊 Tram 1, 2, 5, 13, 14, 17

Oibibio

This department store-cum-spiritual centre (✉ Prins Hendrikkade 20–21) offers a wide range of products made in environmentally friendly ways: clothing in cotton, wool and hemp, natural cosmetics and gifts, including some made from recycled glass, paper and leather. The store includes a bookstore, a café and an entire floor dedicated to workshops and therapy treatments, including yoga, tai chi and shiatsu. You can even learn to play the didgeridoo here.

CLOTHES & ACCESSORIES

CANDY CORSON
One of the best places in Amsterdam for quality leather accessories, especially bags and belts.
🔢 H5 ✉ St Luciensteeg 19 ☎ 6248061 🚋 Trams 13, 14, 17

ESPRIT
Young, trendy designs for the seriously fashionable.
🔢 H5 ✉ Spui 10 ☎ 6221967 🚋 Tram 1, 2, 5

HESTER VAN EEGHEN
Handbags, wallets and other leather accessories in innovative shapes, styles and colours, designed in Holland and made in Italy.
🔢 G5 ✉ Hartenstraat 1 ☎ 6269212 🚋 Tram 13, 14, 17

THE MADHATTER
Hand-made hats by Dutch designers.
🔢 H7 ✉ Van der Heistplein 4 ☎ 6647748 🚋 Tram 3, 4, 16

MEXX
Top designer boutique boasting many of the leading French and Italian labels.
🔢 G6 ✉ P C Hooftstraat 118 ☎ 6750171 🚋 Tram 2, 3, 5, 12

OGER
One of the top menswear boutiques.
🔢 G6 ✉ P C Hooftstraat 81 ☎ 6768695 🚋 Tram 2, 3, 5, 12

OILILY
Children love the brightly coloured and patterned sporty clothes of this Dutch company.
🔢 G6 ✉ P C Hooftstraat 131–133 ☎ 6723361 🚋 Tram 2, 3, 5, 12

OSCAR
You'll find all the latest trends in footwear here, from glittery platforms to psychedelic thigh boots.
🔢 H4 ✉ Nieuwendijk 208–10 ☎ 6253143 🚋 Tram 4, 9, 14, 16, 24, 25

PALETTE
The smallest shop in the Netherlands has the largest selection of silk and satin shoes, available in 500 colours.
🔢 H5 ✉ Nieuwezijds Voorburgwal 125 ☎ 6393207 🚋 Tram 4, 9, 14, 16, 24, 25

PUCK & HANS
The wackier end of high fashion, with designs by Katharine Hamnett, Jean Paul Gaultier and others.
🔢 H5 ✉ Rokin 66 ☎ 6255889 🚋 Tram 1, 2, 5, 13, 17

RETRO
Shop here for way-out fashion, including a dazzling array of sixties and seventies flower-power clothing for adults and children.
🔢 F6 ✉ Constantijn Huygenstraat 57 ☎ 6834180 🚋 Tram 1, 3, 6, 12

SISSY-BOY
This Dutch clothing chain produces smart, affordable clothing for men and women.
🔢 G5 ✉ Leidsestraat 15 ☎ 6238949 🚋 Tram 1, 2, 5

Bargains

There are often excellent bargains to be found in Amsterdam, especially during the sales in January and July. Look out for signs saying *Uitverkoop* (closing-down or end-of-season sale), and *korting* (discounted goods).

THEATRE, DANCE & FILM

THEATRE & DANCE

FELIX MERITIS

An important centre of avant-garde dance and drama, and home to the Shaffy experimental theatre company.

⊞ G5 ⊠ Keizersgracht 324 ☎ 6231311 🚊 Tram 13, 14, 17

DE KLEINE KOMEDIE

The very best in cabaret and stand-up comedy, in one of Amsterdam's oldest theatres.

⊞ H5 ⊠ Amstel 56 ☎ 6240534 🚊 Tram 4, 14, 19

KONINKLIJK THEATER CARRÉ

The 'Royal Theatre' plays host to long-running international musicals, revues, cabaret, folk dancing and an annual Christmas circus.

⊞ H–J6 ⊠ Amstel 115–25 ☎ 6225225 Ⓜ Weesperplein

MUZIEK THEATER (STOPERA)

One of Amsterdam's cultural mainstays (see panel).

⊞ H5 ⊠ Waterlooplein 22 ☎ 6255455 (recorded information in Dutch; hold for operator) Ⓜ Waterlooplein

STADSSCHOUWBURG

Classical and modern plays form the main repertoire of the stylish, 19th-century Municipal Theatre.

⊞ G6 ⊠ Leidseplein 26 ☎ 6242311 🚊 Tram 1, 2, 5, 6, 7, 10

DE STALHOUDERIJ

One of the city's very few English-language theatre companies, located in the city's smallest theatre – a converted stable with seating for 40.

⊞ G5 ⊠ 1e Bloemdwarsstraat 4 ☎ 6262282 🚊 Tram 13, 14, 17

VONDELPARK THEATRE

The open-air theatre in the park offers a programme of drama, cabaret, concerts and children's programmes from June to August.

⊞ F6 ⊠ Vondelpark ☎ 5237700 🚊 Tram 1, 6

FILM

CITY 1–7

Amsterdam's largest multi-screen cinema.

⊞ G6 ⊠ Kleine Gartmanplantsoen 13–25 ☎ 6234579 🚊 Tram 1, 2, 5, 6, 7, 10

FILM MUSEUM CINEMATHEEK

A changing international programme, ranging from silent movies to more recent releases.

⊞ G6 ⊠ Vondelpark 3 ☎ 5891400 🚊 Tram 2, 3, 5, 6, 12

TUCHINSKI CINEMA

Holland's most attractive and prestigious cinema. The classic art deco interior alone makes it worth visiting, no matter what's showing.

⊞ H5 ⊠ Reguliersbreestraat 26 ☎ 6262633 🚊 Tram 4, 9, 14

Subtitles rather than dubbing are used for most non-Dutch films.

Tickets

For theatre information and tickets, contact the AUB (⊠ Leidseplein 26 ☎ 6211211 Ⓜ office open daily 10–6, Thu until 9; telephone answered 9–9 daily). Tickets for most performances can also be purchased from the VVV tourist offices. The daily newspapers and listings magazine *Uitkrant* have programme details.

Muziek Theater (Stopera)

The Municipal Music Theatre, best known as the 'Stopera', has been home to the Dutch national opera and ballet companies since it opened in 1986. Holland's largest auditorium, it seats 1,689 and boasts an internationally famous repertoire as well as putting on experimental works. Guided tours on Wed and Sat at 3PM provide a fascinating glimpse backstage in one of Europe's most up-to-date theatres (➤ 55).

CLASSICAL MUSIC & OPERA

Concertgebouw

Brahms called the Dutch 'schlechte Musikanten' ('dreadful musicians') after visiting Holland in 1879, because there was no satisfactory venue for his music. Thanks to this insult, the magnificent neo-Renaissance Concertgebouw was commissioned embracing the wonderful acoustics that make it a favourite with musicians of international renown. The Royal Concertgebouw Orchestra made its début in 1888, and has since come under the baton of Richard Strauss, Mahler, Ravel, Schönberg and Haitink to name but a few. It continues to be one of the most respected ensembles in the world.

BEURS VAN BERLAGE

Home to the Netherlands Philharmonic Orchestra and Dutch Chamber Orchestra, this remarkable early modernist building once housed the stock exchange, but now makes an impressive concert hall (guided tours only ► 54).
🔲 H4–5 ☒ Damrak 213–279 ☎ 6270466 🚋 Tram 4, 9, 16, 24, 25

CONCERTGEBOUW

One of the world's finest concert halls (see panel).
🔲 G7 ☒ Concertgebouwplein 2–6 ☎ 6718345 🚋 Tram 3, 5, 12, 16

IJSBREKER

A major international venue for contemporary classical music. There are performances of work by John Cage, Xanakis and other modern music pioneers, and around half the concerts are devoted to modern Dutch compositions.
🔲 J6 ☒ Weesperzijde 23 ☎ 6939093 🚇 Weesperplein

MUZIEK THEATER (STOPERA)

Major operatic works and experimental opera from the Dutch National Opera and other leading international companies (► 55 and 77).
🔲 H5 ☒ Waterlooplein 22 ☎ 255455 🚇 Waterlooplein

NIEUWE KERK

Frequent lunchtime concerts and exceptional organ recitals by visiting organists, in an atmospheric setting (► 37).

🔲 H5 ☒ Dam ☎ 6268168 🚋 Tram 1, 2, 4, 5, 9, 13, 14, 16, 17, 24, 25

OUDE KERK

Chamber music concerts and organ recitals are held in this old church, where Holland's foremost composer, Jan Pieters Sweelinck (1562–1621) was once organist. Pass by at 4PM on Saturdays, and you may hear a carillon concert (► 40).
🔲 H5 ☒ Oudekerksplein 23 ☎ 6258284 🚇 Nieuwmarkt

RAI

This convention centre sometimes stages classical music and opera events.
🔲 G–H8 ☒ Europaplein ☎ 5491212 🚋 Tram 4

TROPENMUSEUM

Traditional music from developing countries is performed at the museum's Soeterijn Theatre (► 48).
🔲 K6 ☒ Linnaeusstraat 2 ☎ 5688215 🚋 Tram 6, 9, 10, 14

WESTERGASFABRIEK

A popular venue for experimental opera.
🔲 F3 ☒ Haarlemmerweg 10 ☎ 6211211 🚌 Bus 18, Tram 10

LIVE MUSIC

AKHNATON

Reggae, rap and salsa dance nights in a funky multi-cultural youth centre.

➕ H4 ✉ Nieuwezijds Kolk 25 ☎ 6243396 🚊 Tram 1, 2, 5, 11, 13, 17

ALTO JAZZ CAFÉ

One of Amsterdam's best jazz clubs. Live music nightly, pricey drinks.

➕ G6 ✉ Korte Leidsedwarsstraat 115 ☎ 6263249 🚊 Tram 1, 2, 5, 6, 7, 10

BIMHUIS JAZZ & IMPROVISATION

The place for serious followers of avant garde and experimental jazz, attracting top international players.

➕ H5 ✉ Oudeschans 73 ☎ 6231361 🚇 Nieuwmarkt

BOURBON STREET

Nightly blues and jazz.

➕ G6 ✉ Leidsekruisstraat 6–8 ☎ 6233440 🚊 Tram 6, 7, 10

CANECAO

Brazilian bar with live salsa nightly .

➕ G6 ✉ Lange Leidsedwarsstraat 86 ☎ 6380611 🚊 Tram 6, 7, 10

DE ENGELBE-WAARDER

Relaxed bar, often filled with students, with live jazz on Sundays from 4PM.

➕ H5 ✉ Kloveniersburgwal 59 ☎ 6253772 🚇 Nieuwmarkt

DE HEEREN VAN AEMSTEL

Prior to events such as the North Sea Jazz Festival, you can often see some of the world's great jazz performers here.

➕ H6 ✉ Thorbeckeplein 5 ☎ 6202173 🚊 Tram 4, 9, 14

HOF VAN HOLLAND

Come here for an evening of Dutch folk music and traditional *lieder*.

➕ H5 ✉ Rembrandtplein 5 ☎ 6234650 🚊 Tram 4, 9, 14

JOSEPH LAM JAZZ CAFÉ

This traditional jazz club features live Dixieland on Saturdays.

➕ G3 ✉ Van Diemenstraat 242 ☎ 6228086 🚌 Bus 28

O'REILLY'S IRISH PUB

Choice whiskeys and hearty Irish fare accompanied by jolly folk music.

➕ H5 ✉ Paleisstraat 103–105 ☎ 6249498 🚊 Tram 1, 2, 5

PARADISO

Rock, reggae and pop concerts, in a beautiful old converted church.

➕ G6 ✉ Weteringschans 6–8 ☎ 6264521 🚊 Tram 6, 7, 10

THE STRING

Once a stage for the city's buskers, this intimate bar now offers a programme of blues, jazz and folk music.

➕ H5 ✉ Nes 98 ☎ 6259015 🚊 Tram 4, 9, 14, 16, 24, 25

TWEE ZWAANTJES

Traditional Dutch entertainment off the tourist track: a tiny bar full of accordion-playing, folk-singing Jordaaners.

➕ G4 ✉ Prinsengracht 114 ☎ 6252729 🚊 Tram 13, 14, 17

Melkweg

Located in a wonderful old dairy building (hence the name *Melkweg* or 'Milky Way') on a canal just off Leidseplein, this off-beat arts centre opened in the '60s and remains a shrine to alternative culture. Live bands play in the old warehouse most evenings, and there is also a constantly changing programme of unconventional theatre, dance, art and film events. (✉ Lijnbaansgracht 234 ☎ 6248492).

CAFÉS & BARS

Ancient and modern

Brown cafés, so-called because of their chocolate-coloured walls and dark wooden fittings, are reminiscent of the interiors in Dutch Old Master paintings. Here visitors can meet the locals in a *gezellig* (cosy) atmosphere. In stark contrast, there are a growing number of brasserie-like grand cafés, and chic, modern designer bars, with stylish, spacious interiors. Look out also for the tiny ancient *proeflokalen* tasting bars (originally distillers' private sampling rooms), with ageing barrels and gleaming brass taps, serving a host of gins and liqueurs.

BROWN CAFÉS

FRASCATI
A lively, cultured crowd frequent this bar next to an experimental theatre.
🚇 H5 ✉ Nes 59 ☎ 6241324
🚋 Tram 4, 9, 14, 16, 24, 25

HOPPE
One of Amsterdam's longest-established, most popular brown cafés. Beer in one bar and gin from the barrel in another.
🚇 G5 ✉ Spui 18–20
☎ 4204420 🚋 Tram 1, 2, 5

DE KARPERSHOEK
A sawdust-strewn bar dating from 1629, and frequented by sailors.
🚇 H4 ✉ Martelaarsgracht 2
☎ 6247886 🚉 Centraal Station

HET MOLENPAD
An old-fashioned brown café. The canalside terrace catches the early evening sun.
🚇 G5 ✉ Prinsengracht 653
☎ 6259680 🚋 Tram 1, 2, 5

PAPENEILAND
Amsterdam's oldest bar resembles a scene from a Dutch Old Master painting, with its panelled walls, Makkum tiles, candles, benches and wood-burning stove.
🚇 G4 ✉ Prinsengracht 2
☎ 6241989 🚌 Bus 18, 22, 44

DE PRINS
Very much a locals' bar, despite its proximity to the Anne Frankhuis, with a cosy pub atmosphere and seasonal menu.
🚇 G4 ✉ Prinsengracht 124
☎ 6249382 🚋 Tram 13, 14, 17

VAN PUFFELEN
An intimate sawdust-strewn brown bar with a smart restaurant at the back. You can sit on a barge moored outside, on the Prinsengracht, in summer.
🚇 G5 ✉ Prinsengracht 375–377 ☎ 6246270
🚋 Tram 13, 14, 17

GRAND CAFÉS & DESIGNER BARS

DE JAREN
A spacious, ultra-modern café, known for its trendy clientele and its sunny terraces overlooking the Amstel.
🚇 H5 ✉ Nieuwe Doelenstraat 20–22 ☎ 6255771 🚋 Tram 4, 9, 14, 16, 24, 25

DE KROON
A chic, colonial-style bar, with outsize pot plants and wicker furniture, and an executive clientele.
🚇 H5 ✉ Rembrandtplein 17
☎ 6252011 🚋 Tram 4, 9, 14

HET LAND VAN WALEM
One of Amsterdam's first designer bars.
🚇 G5 ✉ Keizersgracht 449
☎ 6253544 🚋 Tram 1, 2, 5, 11

LUXEMBOURG
Watch the world go by whilst eating canapés or colossal club sandwiches on the terrace of this elegant, high-ceilinged bar.
🚇 G5 ✉ Spui 22–24
☎ 6206264 🚋 Tram 1, 2, 5

L'OPERA
Fashionable with the city's chic set.

➕ H5 ✉ Rembrandtplein 27–31 ☎ 6275232 🚋 Tram 4, 9, 14

SCHILLER

An evocative art deco bar with live piano music.
➕ H5 ✉ Rembrandtplein 26 ☎ 6249846 🚋 Tram 4, 9, 14

PROEFLOKALEN (TASTING BARS)

CAFÉ HOOGHOUDT

Brown bar-cum-*proeflokalen* in an old warehouse lined with stoneware *jenever* barrels. Tasty Dutch appetisers and a huge selection of liqueurs. Ask for the barman's recommendation.
➕ H6 ✉ Reguliersgracht 11 ☎ 4204041 🕐 Noon–1AM 🚋 Tram 4, 9, 14, 16, 24, 25

DE DRIE FLESCHJES

Amsterdammers have been tasting gins in 'The Three Little Bottles' since 1650.
➕ H5 ✉ Gravenstraat 18 ☎ 6248443 🚋 Tram 1, 2, 4, 5, 9, 13, 14, 16, 17, 24, 25

DE OOIEVAAR

A homely atmosphere pervades 'The Stork', one of Holland's smallest *proeflokalen*.
➕ H4 ✉ Sint Olofspoort 1 ☎ 4208004 🕐 Centraal Station

SPECIALIST BARS

DE BEIAARD

A beer-drinker's paradise – over 40 beers from around the world.
➕ G5 ✉ Spui 30 ☎ 6225110 🚋 Tram 1, 2, 5,

BROUWERIJ'T IJ

A bar inside the old De Gooier windmill (▶ 60), serving lethally strong beer brewed on the premises.
➕ K5 ✉ Funenkade 7 ☎ 6228325 🕐 Fri–Sun 3PM–8PM 🚌 Bus 22, 28

BULLDOG PALACE

Flagship of the famous 'Bulldog Empire' of alternative culture – a plush, loud bar, brashly decked out in stars and stripes. Downstairs is a 'smoking coffeeshop' (▶ 69).
➕ G6 ✉ Leidseplein 13–17 ☎ 6271908 🚋 Tram 1, 2, 5, 6, 7, 10

CYBER C@FÉ

The first of several internet cafés now open in Amsterdam. Also a 'smoking coffeeshop' (▶ 69).
➕ H4 ✉ Nieuwendijk 19 ☎ 6235146 (e-mail: visitor1@cybercafe.euronet.nl) 🕐 Centraal Station

HARD ROCK CAFÉ

One of three of this ubiquitous chain in Amsterdam. This is the most central and atmospheric, and has a Hard Rock Café shop next door.
➕ H5 ✉ Oudezijds Voorburgwal 246 ☎ 6253180 🕐 Nieuwmarkt

HARRY'S AMERICAN BAR

A sophisticated cocktail bar.
➕ G5 ✉ Spuistraat 285 ☎ 6244384 🕐 Evenings and Sun brunch only 🚋 Tram 1, 2, 5

Bar talk

Most of the 1,402 bars and cafés in Amsterdam are open from around 10AM until the early hours and most serve meals. *Proeflokalen* open from around 4PM until 8PM, and some serve snacks, such as nuts, cheese, meatballs and sausage. Beer is the most popular alcoholic drink. It is always served with a head, and often with a *jenever* chaser called a *kopstoot* (a blow to the head). If you want only a small beer, ask for a *Kleintje pils*. Dutch for 'cheers' is *Proost!*

'Dutch courage'

Dutch gin (*jenever*), made from molasses and flavoured with juniper berries, comes in a variety of ages: *jong* (young), *oud* (old) and *zeer oud* (the oldest and the mellowest). Other flavours may be added. After a glass or two of *bessenjenever* (blackcurrant), *bitterkoekjes likeur* (macaroon) or just straight *jenever*, you may have a new insight into the meaning of Dutch courage.

NIGHTCLUBS

Gay Amsterdam

Clubbing is at the heart of Amsterdam's gay scene. The best-known venue is iT, a glitzy disco with throbbing techno sounds. Gay bars and clubs abound in nearby Reguliersdwarsstraat and Halvemaansteeg. To find out exactly what's on and where it's happening, call the Gay and Lesbian Switchboard (☎ 6236565) or read the English-language *Guide for Gays* magazine.

DANSEN BIJ JANSEN
Informal student disco, playing all the latest chart toppers.
✚ H5 ✉ Handboogstraat 11
☎ 6201779 🕐 11PM–4:30AM
🚋 Tram 1, 2, 5,

ESCAPE
Amsterdam's largest disco can hold 2,000 dancers. Dazzling light show, superb sound system.
✚ H5 ✉ Rembrandtplein 11–15 ☎ 6223542 🕐 10PM–4AM (Fri & Sat until 5AM)
🚋 Tram 4, 9, 14

iT
Without doubt the wildest disco in town, with outrageously dressed (or rather undressed) clientele and fierce house music. Saturday night is exclusively gay.
✚ H5 ✉ Amstelstraat 24
☎ 6250111 🕐 11PM–4AM.
Closed Sun–Wed 🚋 Tram 9, 14

JULIANA'S
Attracts an older crowd looking for a quieter club atmosphere.
✚ F7 ✉ Hiton Hotel, Apollolaan 24 ☎ 6780780
🚋 Tram 16

MAZZO
A young, image-conscious crowd prop up the bar of this small, trendy disco in the Jordaan, while guest DJs and live bands play the latest sounds.
✚ G5 ✉ Rozengracht 114
☎ 6267500 🕐 11PM–4AM, Sat until 5AM 🚋 Tram 13, 14, 17

NAAR BOVEN
A café-cum-nightclub with live music from jazz and blues to rock and house.
✚ H5 ✉ Reguliersdwarsstraat 12 ☎ 6233981 🚋 Tram 4, 9, 14, 16, 24, 25

ODEON
This converted canal house caters for all tastes: house music on the ground floor, 60s–80s classic disco upstairs and jazz in the basement.
✚ H5 ✉ Singel 460
☎ 6249711 🕐 10PM–4AM (Fri & Sat until 5AM) 🚋 Tram 1, 2, 5

(OP DE SCHAAL VAN) RICHTER 36
Seismic atmosphere is promised at the '36 on the Richter Scale' nightclub, with its earthquake-inspired decor. The most popular disco in town.
✚ H5 ✉ Reguliersdwarsstraat 36 ☎ 6261573
🕐 midnight–4:30AM 🚋 Tram 1, 2, 5, 16, 24, 25

ROXY
This cool club in an old cinema is a favourite with Amsterdam's chic club-set.
✚ H5 ✉ Singel 465–467
☎ 6200354 🕐 11PM–4AM (Fri & Sat until 5AM) 🚋 Tram 1, 2, 4, 5, 9, 14, 24, 25

SOUL KITCHEN
Amsterdam's leading 'non-house' club consequently attracts a slightly older clientele.
✚ H5 ✉ Amstelstraat 32
☎ 6202333 🕐 Wed–Sun 11PM–4AM (Fri until 5AM)
🚋 Tram 9, 14

SEYMOUR LIKELY 2
Jazz dance, soul, disco and hip-hop in trendy 'post-nuclear-fall out' surroundings.
✚ H5 ✉ Nieuwezijds Voorburgwal 161 ☎ 4205062
🚋 Tram 1, 2, 5, 13, 17

SPORT

FISHING

Obtain a permit from the Dutch Fishing Federation to fish in the Amsterdamse Bos.

➕ H6 ✉ Nicolaas Witsenstraat 10 ☎ 6264988 🚊 Tram 6, 7, 10

FITNESS

JANSEN AEROBIC FITNESSCENTRUM

Fitness centre with gyms, sauna, solarium and daily aerobics classes.

➕ H5 ✉ Rokin 109 ☎ 6269366 🚊 Tram 4, 9, 14, 16, 24, 25

GAMBLING

HOLLAND CASINO

One of Europe's largest casinos

➕ G6 ✉ Max Euweplein 62 ☎ 6201006 🚊 Tram 1, 2, 5, 6, 7, 10

GO-KARTING

KAARTBAAN

Fun for both adults and children.

➕ B3 ✉ Theemsweg 19 ☎ 6111642 🚊 Train to Sloterdijk

GOLF

GOLFBAAN WATERLAND

New 18-hole course just north of the city centre.

➕ L1 ✉ Buikslotermeerdijk 141 ☎ 6361010

HORSE-RIDING

HOLLANDSE MANEGE

Amsterdam's most central riding school.

➕ F6 ✉ Vondelstraat 140 ☎ 6180942 🚊 Tram 1, 6

JOGGING

There are marked trails through the Vondelpark and Amsterdamse Bos.

For serious runners, the Amsterdam Marathon is in May, and the Grachtenloop canal race in June (▶ 22), when up to 5,000 people choose to run either 5, 10 or 20km along the banks of Prinsengraacht and Vijzelgracht.

ICE-SKATING

In early November, the café terrace in Leidseplein is transformed into an open-air ice-rink.

JAAP EDEN BAAN

A large indoor ice-rink, open October to March.

➕ L7 ✉ Radioweg 64 ☎ 6949652 🚊 Tram 9

SWIMMING

In summer head to the seaside, only 20 minutes away by train, with miles of clean, sandy beaches. Try Zandvoort, Bergan or Noordwijk.

MIRANDA BAD

Sub-tropical swimming pool complex, with indoor and outdoor pools, a beach and wave machines.

➕ H8 ✉ De Mirandalaan 9 ☎ 6428080 🚊 Tram 25

TENNIS

AMSTELPARK TENNIS CENTRE

Holland's biggest tennis school.

➕ F9 ✉ Karel Lotsylaan 8 ☎ 6445436 🚊 V.U.

WATERSPORTS

DUIKELAAR, SLOTERPARK

A water park with sailing boats, canoes and sail-boards to rent in summer.

➕ C5 ✉ Noordzijde 41 ☎ 6138855 🚊 Tram 14

Spectator sports

Football is Holland's number one spectator sport and the number one team is Ajax Amsterdam. Watch them play at home, at Middenweg 401 (☎ 6946515). Other popular events include international hockey at Wagenaar Stadium (✉ Nieuwe Kalfjeslaan ☎ 6401141) and show-jumping at RAI (✉ Europaplein ☎ 5491212) every November. Look out for a Dutch hybrid of volleyball and netball called *korfball*, and *carambole* – billiards on a table without pockets.

LUXURY HOTELS

Prices

Expect to pay over f400 a night for a double room in a luxury hotel.

'Tradition meets excellence'

'Tradition meets excellence' is the motto of Holland's most luxurious and most expensive hotel, the Amstel Inter-Continental, situated beside the Amstel River. It has recently been refurbished for f70 million, and its stately grandeur and opulent decor are overwhelming. It does lie a little way from the centre, but the hotel provides a motor yacht and luxury limousines to make sightseeing easier. Splash out and join the countless kings, queens, stars and rich tourists who have stayed here.

AMERICAN
A classic Amsterdam hotel on the Leidseplein, built in resplendent art nouveau style.
➕ G6 ✉ Leidsekade 97
☎ 6245322 🚋 Tram 1, 2, 5, 6, 7, 10

AMSTEL INTER-CONTINENTAL
Amsterdam's flagship hotel set beside the Amstel River (see panel).
➕ J6 ✉ Prof Tulpplein 1
☎ 6226060 🚋 Tram 6, 7, 10

BILDERBERG GARDEN
Pleasantly situated in a leafy suburb but just a short tram ride from the city centre.
➕ F7 ✉ Dijsselhofplantsoen 7
☎ 6642121 🚋 Tram 16

DE L'EUROPE
A prestigious 5-star de luxe hotel, combining Victorian elegance with modern comfort and world-class *haute cuisine*.
➕ H5 ✉ Nieuwe Doelenstraat 2–8 ☎ 6234836 🚋 Tram 4, 6, 9, 14, 16, 24, 25

GOLDEN TULIP BARBIZON PALACE
Modern luxury deftly concealed within a row of 17th-century mansions. Many rooms are split-level suites and have ancient oak beams.
➕ H4 ✉ Prins Hendrikkade 59–72 ☎ 5564564
🚇 Centraal Station

GRAND
Once a 16th-century royal inn, then the City Hall, this magnificent historic building is now a luxury hotel.
➕ H5 ✉ Oudezijds Voorburgwal 197 ☎ 5553111
🚇 Nieuwmarkt

GRAND HOTEL KRASNAPOLSKY
Previous guests at this centrally located luxury hotel have included Brahms, Conrad, Mahler, the Rolling Stones and President Mitterrand.
➕ H5 ✉ Dam 9
☎ 5549111 🚋 Tram 1, 2, 4, 5, 9, 13, 14, 16, 17, 24, 25

HILTON
In 1969 the honeymoon suite was the scene of John Lennon and Yoko Ono's week-long 'love-in' for world peace. It is decorated with words from *All You Need is Love* and *Imagine*.
➕ F7 ✉ Apollolaan 138–140
☎ 6780780 🚋 Tram 16

MARRIOTT
Ideally sited within easy walking distance of Amsterdam's main museums, shops and nightlife centres.
➕ G6 ✉ Stadhouderskade 19–21 ☎ 6075555 🚋 Tram 1, 2, 5, 6

PULITZER
Twenty-four 17th-century houses, once the homes of wealthy merchants, have been converted into this luxurious canalside hotel.
➕ G5 ✉ Prinsengracht 315–331 ☎ 5235235
🚋 Tram 13, 14, 17

RENAISSANCE
A modern hotel, perfect for business or pleasure, just a stone's throw from Dam and Centraal Station.
➕ H4 ✉ Kattengat 1
☎ 6212223 🚋 Tram 13, 14, 17

MID-RANGE HOTELS

AMBASSADE
Amsterdam's smartest B&B, in a series of characterful, gabled canal houses.
➕ G5 ✉ Herengracht 335–353 ☎ 6262333 🚋 Tram 1, 2, 5

AMSTERDAM
A traditional hotel right at the heart of Amsterdam's business and entertainment centre.
➕ H5 ✉ Damrak 93–94 ☎ 5550666 🚋 Tram 4, 9, 14, 16, 24, 25

CANAL HOUSE
Antique furnishings and a pretty garden make this small, family-run hotel, set on the Keizersgracht an absolute gem.
➕ G4 ✉ Keizersgracht 148 ☎ 6225182 🚋 Tram 13, 14, 17

LA CASALO
Amsterdam's smallest hotel – a converted houseboat with only four guest rooms.
➕ J7 ✉ Amsteldijk 862 ☎ 6423680 🚋 Tram 4

DOELEN KARENA HOTEL
Amsterdam's oldest hotel, celebrated as the place where Rembrandt painted the '*Night Watch*'.
➕ H5 ✉ Nieuwe Doelenstraat 24 ☎ 6220722 🚋 Tram 4, 9, 14, 16, 24, 25

EUREKA
A small, quiet 3-star hotel on the Amstel, suitable for tourists and business users alike.
➕ H5 ✉ 'S-Gravelandseveer 3–4 ☎ 6246607 🚋 Tram 4, 9, 14, 16, 24, 25

JAN LUYKEN
A well-run, elegant town-house hotel in a quiet back-street near Vondelpark and the Museumplein.
➕ G6 ✉ Jan Luijkenstraat 58 ☎ 5730730 🚋 Tram 2, 3, 5, 12

MAAS
A charming, family-run, waterfront hotel; round the corner from Leidseplein and ideally positioned for exploring Amsterdam's museums, shops and nightlife. Ask for a waterbed!
➕ G6 ✉ Leidsekade 91 ☎ 6233868 🚋 Tram 1, 2, 5, 6, 7, 10

PRINSENGRACHT
A small three-star hotel, with a garden and 34 rooms, on one of the most beautiful canals.
➕ H6 ✉ Prinsengracht 1015 ☎ 6237779 🚋 Tram 4

REMBRANDT RESIDENCE
Stay on Amsterdam's most celebrated canal to appreciate the real atmosphere of the city.
➕ G5 ✉ Herengracht 255 ☎ 6221727 🚋 Tram 13, 14, 17

TULIP INN
The newest 3-star hotel, in a strikingly modern Amsterdam School-style building. Good facilities for visitors with disabilities.
➕ G5 ✉ Spuistraat 288–292 ☎ 4204545 🚋 Tram 1, 2, 5

Prices
Expect to pay from f200 to f400 a night for a double room in a mid-range hotel

Bed, breakfast, apartments and boats
If you are looking for self-catering accommodation in Amsterdam, contact Amsterdam House (✉ Amstel 176a ☎ 6262577) for a choice of luxury apartments in converted canal houses in the city centre, or even a houseboat. Bed and Breakfast Holland (✉ Theophile de Bockstraat 3, ☎ 6157527) offers the chance to meet the city folk by staying in a private house.

BUDGET ACCOMMODATION

Prices

Expect to pay up to f200 a night for a double room in a budget hotel. Hostels and campsites are considerably cheaper.

Camping

There are several campsites in and around Amsterdam. The best-equipped one is rather a long way out, in the Amsterdamse Bos (✉ Kleine Noorddijk 1, ☎ 6416868). Vliegenbos is just a ten-minute bus ride from the station, close to the River IJ (✉ Meeuwenlaan 138, ☎ 6368855). Contact the VVV for full details.

ACACIA

A cheap, cheerful, family-run hotel in the Jordaan, with self-catering studios and a houseboat which sleeps four.

✚ G4 ✉ Lindengracht 251 ☎ 6221460 🚋 Tram 3

AGORA

A small, comfortable, 18th-century canal house furnished with antiques and filled with flowers from the nearby Bloemenmarkt.

✚ H5 ✉ Singel 462 ☎ 6272200 🚋 Tram 4, 9, 14, 16, 24, 25

AMSTEL BOTEL

One of Amsterdam's few floating hotels, with magnificent views over the old docks.

✚ J4 ✉ Oosterdokskade 2–4 ☎ 6264247 🚌 Bus 22, 39

ARENA 'SLEEP IN'

A large hostel combined with an information centre on youth culture and tourism for independent travellers, especially the young. It has a café and restaurant (with garden terrace), and sometimes holds dance nights, musical performances, exhibitions and other events.

✚ J6 ✉ Gravesandestraat 51 ☎ 6947441 🚋 Tram 3, 6

DE FILOSOOF

Each room in this unique hotel is named after the world's greatest philosophers and decorated accordingly.

✚ F6 ✉ Anna van der Vondelstraat 6 ☎ 6833013 🚋 Tram 1, 6

HOKSEBERGEN

A basic one-star hotel in a characterful, old canal house, within easy walking distance of all the main city sights.

✚ G5 ✉ Singel 301 ☎ 6266043 🚋 Tram 1, 2, 5

JEUGDHERBERG VONDELPARK

Advanced booking and a youth hostel pass are essential here.

✚ G6 ✉ Zandpad 5 ☎ 6831744 🚋 Tram 1, 2, 5, 6

NOVA

A clean, simple, centrally placed hotel, managed by friendly young staff.

✚ H5 ✉ Nieuwezijds Voorburgwal 272–280 ☎ 6230066 🚋 Tram 1, 2, 5

OWL

Ideal for children, near Vondelpark and with a generous garden.

✚ G6 ✉ Roemer Visscherstraat 1 ☎ 6189484 🚋 Tram 2, 3, 5, 12

PRINSENHOF

A quaint, comfortable, clean, canalside B&B. One of the city's best budget options.

✚ H6 ✉ Prinsengracht 810 ☎ 6231772 🚋 Tram 4

VAN OSTADE

A 'bicycle hotel' in the De Pijp district, renting bikes and giving advice on how to discover hidden Amsterdam.

✚ H7 ✉ Van Ostadestraat 123 ☎ 6793452 🚋 Tram 3, 12, 24, 25

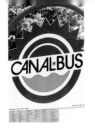

AMSTERDAM
travel facts

ARRIVING & DEPARTING

Before you go

- EU nationals and citizens of the USA, Canada, Australia and New Zealand need a valid passport or national identity card to stay for up to three months. Other nationals require a visa.
- There are no vaccination requirements.

When to go

- Most tourists visit between April and September.
- From late March until late May is the best time to see Holland's bulbfields.
- June, July and August are the sunniest months, but you can never be sure of good weather. Many people visit in June for the Holland Festival.
- In winter, temperatures can drop so low that the canals freeze over. Nevertheless, Christmas is always a busy tourist season.

Arriving by air

- Amsterdam has one international airport (Schiphol), which is 18km from the city centre. Many international airlines operate scheduled and charter flights here, including British Airways, Air UK, British Midlands, Aer Lingus and the Dutch national carrier, KLM.
- Airport information ☎ 06/35034050.
- Trains leave the airport for Amsterdam Centraal Station every 15 minutes from 6AM until midnight, then run hourly through the night. The journey takes 20 minutes and the return fare costs f10.25.
- A taxi from Schiphol Airport to the centre of Amsterdam costs around f70.

Arriving by sea and rail

- The major ferry ports, Vlissingen, Rotterdam and Hook of Holland, have good rail connections with Amsterdam. Regular sailings from the United Kingdom are offered by Stena, Scandinavian Seaways and North Sea Ferries.
- There are good rail connections with most European cities.
- Railway information ☎ 06/9292.

Arriving by car

- Remember to drive on the right.
- Amsterdam is well served by motorways. From the A10 ring road, S-routes (indicated by blue signs) take you into the city centre.
- In the city centre, many streets are one-way, particularly in the canal area. Watch out for cyclists and trams.
- Street parking is very difficult in the city centre. It is metered from 9AM to 7PM and expensive (f2–4 per hour). Use car parks instead.
- Always lock your car securely, and never leave valuables in it.

Customs regulations

- EU nationals are not required to declare items intended for personal use.
- For non-EU nationals the limits are: 200 cigarettes or 50 cigars or 250g of tobacco; 1 litre spirits or 2 litres fortified wine or 2 litres non-sparkling wine; 50ml perfume, 500g coffee and 100g tea plus other goods to the value of f200.

Departing

- Airport tax is included in the price of your ticket.
- There are numerous duty-free shops at Schiphol Airport.

ESSENTIAL FACTS

Electricity
- 220 volts; round two-pin sockets. Take an adapter with you.

Etiquette
- Shake hands on introduction. Once you know people better, you might exchange three pecks on alternate cheeks instead.
- Remember to say *hallo* and *dag* (goodbye) when shopping, and *eet smakelijk* (enjoy your meal) when eating.
- Dress is generally informal, except for the opera, ballet and some theatres.
- Don't walk in cycle lanes (*fietspaden*).
- Although service charges are included in bills, tipping is customary. Round off bills to the nearest guilder, or five guilders for larger bills.

Insurance
- Take out a comprehensive policy before you leave home.

Women travellers
- There are no particular risks for women travelling alone. For information and advice contact the Vrouwenhuil (Women's House) ✉ Nieuwe Herengracht 95 ☎ 6252066
- 'Women Call Women' helpline ☎ 6250105

Money matters
- The guilder (formerly called the florin) is abbreviated in numerous ways: f, fl, Hfl, Dfl, NLG. 1 guilder=100 cents.
- Major credit cards are accepted in most hotels, shops and restaurants.
- Banks usually offer a better exchange rate than hotels or independent bureaux de change. GWK offer 24-hour money-changing services at Schiphol Airport and Centraal Station.
- Embossed symbols on notes enable blind and partially sighted people to identify their value.

National holidays
- 1 January, Good Friday, Easter Sunday and Monday, 30 April, Ascension Day, Whit Sunday and Monday, 25 December and 26 December
  4 and 5 May are Commemoration Days but not public holidays.

Opening hours
- Banks: Mon–Fri 9–4/5. Some stay open Thu until 7.
- Shops: Tue–Sat 9/10–6, Mon 1–6. Some open Thu until 9. Some close early Sat, at 4/5.
- State-run museums and galleries: most open Tue–Sat 10–5, Sun and national holidays 1–5. Many close on Mon.

Places of worship
- Roman Catholic: St John & St Ursula (✚ H5 ✉ Begijnhof 30 ☎ 6221918)
- English Reformed Church: (✚ H5 ✉ Begijnhof 48 ☎ 6249665)
- Jewish: Jewish and Liberal Community Amsterdam: (✚ H9 ✉ Jacob Soetendorpstraat 8 ☎ 6423562)
- Muslim: THAIBA Islamic Cultural Centre: (✚ Off map ✉ Kraaiennest 125 ☎ 6982526)

Student travellers
- Students under 26 can obtain an International Young Person's Passport (CJP – Cultureel Jongeren Passpoort), which gives discounts at some museums, galleries, theatres, restaurants and hotels. It costs f20, from: AUB ✉ Leidseplein 26 ☎ 2611211, and NBBS ✉ Leidststraat 53 ☎ 6381736.

Time differences

- Amsterdam observes Central European Time, 1 hour ahead of Greenwich Mean Time in winter and 2 hours in summer.

Toilets

- There are few public toilets. Use the facilities in hotels, museums and cafés. There is often a small charge.

Tourist offices (VVV)

- The five main VVV offices all have multi-lingual staff, city maps and brochures. They will also make hotel, excursion, theatre and concert reservations for a small fee. They are:
  Centraal Station VVV
  (✚ H4 ✉ Centraal Station)
  Stationsplein VVV
  (✚ H4 ✉ Stationsplein 10)
  Leidseplein VVV
  (✚ G6 ✉ Leidseplein 1)
  Stadionplein VVV
  (✚ E8 ✉ Van Tuyll Van Serooskerkenweg 125)
  and at Schiphol Airport (✚ Y12).
- For telephone enquiries call ☎ 06/34043066.

Visitors with disabilities

- Facilities for the disabled, especially in the hotels and museums along the canals, are not particularly good. It is advisable to check what is available at tourist attractions, theatres and restaurants in advance.
- VVV brochures include details of hotels and tourist attractions with access and facilities for people with disabilities.
- SGOA (Stichting Gehandicapten Overleg Amsterdam) provide comprehensive details on suitable accommodation (✚ G6 ✉ Keizersgracht 523 ☎ 6383838).
- There is a special taxi service for wheelchair users ☎ 6134134.

PUBLIC TRANSPORT

How to use the buses and trams

- The majority of buses and trams start from Centraal Station.
- Seventeen different tram lines run frequently from 6AM on weekdays (slightly later at weekends) until midnight when night buses take over, running hourly until 4AM. Day tickets are valid during the night following the day on which they are issued.
- If you need a ticket, board at the front and pay the driver.
- Take care when getting off. Many stops are in the middle of the road.

How to use the Metro/Light Rail

- There are only three lines, all terminating at Centraal Station. They are used mainly by commuters and, with only four stops in the city centre, are not much use for tourists.

Buying and using tickets

- The GVB (Transport Authority) network is divided into zones.
- The same ticket system is valid for tram, bus and Metro.
- If you intend to use public transport frequently, buy a strip of 15 tickets (*strippenkaart*), available at GVB ticket counters and the VVV. For each journey, a ticket must be stamped for each zone you want to pass through, plus one for the journey: for example, from Centraal station to Leidseplein is two zones, so you need to stamp two tickets of your strippenkaart, plus one more. Zones are shown on maps at tram, bus and Metro stops.
- On buses: tell the driver the number of zones you want and your ticket will be stamped.
- On the Metro or light railway: before boarding, fold back the

appropriate number of strips and punch your ticket in the waist-high yellow ticket machines on the station.

- On trams: either ask the driver to stamp your ticket or do it yourself in a yellow punching-machine. Some trams have a conductor at the back who sells and stamps tickets.

- For a single trip, purchase a 'one-hour' ticket, from the driver of the bus or tram, or from a machine at the Metro entrance. Buy day and other tickets, 2-, 3- and 8-strip cards from VVV offices, news-agents and bus/tram drivers.

- All tickets are valid for one hour, and include transfers.

- Don't travel without a valid ticket! You could be fined f60 plus the ticket price.

- For further information and maps, contact GVB (✚ H4 ✉ Stationsplein ☎ 069292)

Getting around by bicycle

- Without doubt, the best way to see Amsterdam is by bicycle. To hire one costs from f10 a day, f50 a week.
 Damstraat Rent-a-Bike (✚ H5 Pieter Jacobsdwarsstraat 11 ☎ 6255029 ◉ Daily 9–6)
 Bikes-a-Gogo (✚ G5 ✉ Elandsstraat 111 ☎ 6277726 ◉ Daily 9–6)

Taxis

- It is difficult to hail a taxi in the street. Go to a taxi rank outside major hotels, tourist attractions and Centraal Station.

- Fares are high, so add only a small tip.

- Taxicentrale (☎ 6777777) runs a reli-able 24-hour service.

- To travel in style, hail a Water Taxi or order one from the Water Taxi Centrale (✚ H4 ✉ Stationsplein 8 ☎ 6222181)

MEDIA & COMMUNICATIONS

Mail

- Postage to European destinations costs f1 for letters up to 20g, and 80 cents for postcards. Other des-tinations cost slightly more.

- Purchase stamps (*postzegels*) at post offices, tobacconists and sou-venir shops.

- Post boxes are bright red and clearly marked 'ptt post'.

Post offices

- Most post offices open weekdays 8.30 /9–5.

- Main Post Office: ✚ G5
 ✉ Hoofdpostkantoor PTT, Singel 250–256
 ☎ 5563311 ◉ Mon–Fri 9–6, Sat 9–1

- Postal Information: ☎ 06/0417

Telephones

- Most public telephones take phonecards, costing f10 or f25, available from telephone centres, post offices and railway stations.

- Phone calls within Europe cost about f1 per minute.

- Directory enquiries: ☎ 06/8008

- International directory enquiries: ☎ 06/0418

- Numbers starting 06 are premium rate calls.

- Local and international operator: ☎ 06/0410

- To phone abroad, dial 00 followed by the country code (UK 44, USA and Canada 1, Australia 61, New Zealand 64), then the number.

- Cheap rates: UK and Ireland 8AM–8PM and weekends; USA and Canada 7PM–10AM and week-ends; Australia and New Zealand midnight–7AM, 3–8PM and week-ends.

- Most hotels have International Direct Dialling, but it is expensive.

- At the Telecenter (✚ G5 ✉ Raadhuisstraat 48), you can make

91

local, national and international calls and pay afterwards with cash, credit card, traveller's cheque or Eurocheque.

Newspapers and magazines

- The main Dutch newspapers are *De Telegraaf* (right wing), *De Volkskrant* (left wing) and *NRC Handelsblad*.
- The main Amsterdam news-papers (sold nationwide) are *Het Parool* and *Nieuws van de Dag*.
- *Vrij Nederland* is a (very popular, left-wing) weekly news magazine.
- Listings magazines: *What's on in Amsterdam*, *Agenda* and *Uitkrant*.
- International newspapers are available at main kiosks, news-agents and bookshops.

Radio and television

- News is broadcast on Dutch Radio 1 (747kHz), classical music on Radio 4 (98.9mhz) and pop on Radio 3 (96.8mhz). BBC Radio 4 (long wave) is on 198kHzAM and the World Service (medium wave) is on 648kHzAM.
- There are five main Dutch TV channels and numerous cable and satellite stations, including French, German and Italian stations, BBC1 and 2, NBC Superchannel, CNN and MTV.

EMERGENCIES

Emergency phone numbers

- Police: ☎ 06 11 or 6 22 22 22
- Ambulance: ☎ 06 11 or 5 55 55 55
- Fire Service: ☎ 06 11 or 6 21 21 21
- Tourist Medical Service: ☎ 6245793 (day), 5923355 (24hr)
- Automobile Emergency (ANWB): ☎ 06 08 88
- Lost credit cards: American Express ☎ 5048666, Diners Club ☎ 5573557, Master/Eurocard ☎ 030/2836000, Visa ☎ 6600611

- Sexual Abuse (◉ 24 hours): ☎ 6387636
- Crisis Helpline (◉ Mon–Thu 9AM–3AM, Fri–Sun 24 hours) ☎ 6 75 75 75

Embassies and consulates

- British Consulate: ✚ F7 ✉ Koningslaan 44 ☎ 6764343
- American Consulate: ✚ G6 ✉ Museumplein 19 ☎ 6645661
- Canadian Embassy: ✉ Sophianlaan 7, The Hague ☎ 070/3111600
- Australian Embassy: ✉ Koninginnegracht, The Hague ☎ 070/3108200
- New Zealand Embassy: ✉ Carnegielaan 10, The Hague ☎ 070/3469324

Lost Property

- For insurance purposes, report lost or stolen property to the police as soon as possible.
- Main lost property offices: Centraal Station (✚ H4 ✉ Stationsplein 15 ☎ 5578544 ◉ 7AM–11PM daily); Police Lost Property (✚ K7 ✉ Steffersonstraat ☎ 5593005 ◉ Mon–Fri noon–3.30)
- For property lost on public transport, GVB (✚ H4 ✉ Prins Hendrikkade 108–14 ☎ 5514408 ◉ Mon–Fri 9–4)

Medicines

- For non-prescription drugs, plas-ters and so on, go to a *drogist*.
- For prescription medicines, go to an *apotheek*, open Mon–Fri 8:30–5:30.
- Details of pharmacies open out-side normal hours are in the daily newspaper *Het Parool* and all pharmacy windows.
- The Central Medical Service (☎ 06/35032042) can refer you to a duty GP or dentist.
- Hospital outpatient clinics are open 24 hours a day. The most central is Onze Lieve Vrouwe Gasthuis (✚ J6 ✉ 1e Oosterparkstraat 279 ☎ 5999111 ◉ Trams 3, 6, 10)
- For an ambulance call 06 11.

Crime

- Pickpockets abound in busy shopping streets and markets, and in the Red Light District. Take sensible precautions and remain on your guard at all times.
- At night, avoid poorly lit areas and keep to busy streets. Amsterdam is not a dangerous city, but muggings do occur.

LANGUAGE

Basics

yes	ja
no	nee
please	alstublieft
thank you	Dank u
hello	hallo
good morning	goedemorgen
good afternoon	goedemiddag
good evening	goedenavond
good night	slaap lekker
goodbye	dag
breakfast	het ontbijt

Useful words

good/bad	goed/slecht
big/small	groot/klein
hot/cold	warm/koud
new/old	nieuw/oud
open/closed	open/gesloten
push/pull	duwen/trekken
entrance/exit	ingang/uitgang
men's/women's toilet	heren/damen wc
free/occupied	vrij/bezet
far/near	ver/dichtbij
left/right	links/rechts
straight on	rechtdoor

Restaurant

breakfast	het ontbijt
lunch	de lunch
dinner	het diner
menu	de kaart
winelist	de wijnkaart
main course	het hoofdgerecht
dessert	het nagerect
the bill, please	mag ik afrekenen

Numbers

1	een	15	vijftien
2	twee	16	zestien
3	drie	17	zeventien
4	vier	18	achtien
5	vijf	19	negentien
6	zes	20	twintig
7	zeven	21	eenentwintig
8	acht	22	tweeentwintig
9	negen	30	dertig
10	tien	40	veertig
11	elf	50	vijftig
12	twaalf	100	hondert
13	dertien	1,000	duizend
14	veertien		

Days and times

Sunday	Zondag
Monday	Maandag
Tuesday	Dinsdag
Wednesday	Woensdag
Thursday	Donderdag
Friday	Vrijdag
Saturday	Zaterdag
today	vandaag
yesterday	gisteren
tomorrow	morgen

Useful phrases

Do you speak English? Spreekt u engels?

Do you have a vacant room? Zijn er nog kamers vrij?

with bath/shower met bad/douche

I don't understand Ik snap het niet

I'm sorry Sorry

Where is/are …? Waar is/zijn …?

How far is it to …? Hoe ver is het naar …?

How much does this cost? Hoeveel kost dit? …

Do you take (credit cards/traveller's cheques)? Neemt u (credit cards/reischeques) ann?

What time do you open? Hoe laat gaat u open?

What time do you close? How laat gaat u dicht?

Can you help me? Kunt u mij halpen?

93

INDEX

CityPack
Amsterdam

Written by   Teresa Fisher
Edited, designed and produced by
   AA Publishing
Maps   © The Automobile Association 1997
Fold-out map © RV Reise- und Verkehrsverlag Munich · Stuttgart
   © Cartography: GeoData

Distributed in the United Kingdom by AA Publishing, Norfolk House, Priestley Road, Basingstoke, Hampshire, RG24 9NY.

A CIP catalogue record for this book is available from the British Library.

ISBN 0 7495 1520 1

Published by AA Publishing (a trading name of Automobile Association Developments Limited, whose registered office is Norfolk House, Priestley Road, Basingstoke, Hampshire RG24 9NY. Registered number 1878835).

Colour separation by Daylight Colour Art Pte Ltd, Singapore
Printed and bound by Dai Nippon Printing Co (Hong Kong) Ltd.

Acknowledgements
Teresa Fisher wishes to thank the Netherlands Board of Tourism, the VVV, British Midland, Air UK, Hotel Maas, Hotel Nova, Damstraat Rent-a-Bike and Bikes-a-Gogo for their assistance in preparing this book.
The Automobile Assoication wishes to thank the following photographers, libraries and museums for their assistance in the preparation of this book: Anne Frankhuis 31a; Mary Evans Picture Library 38b; Museum het Rembrandthuis 44a, 44b; Museum Willet-Holthuysen 42; Eddy Posthuma de Boer 31b, 39, 46; Rex Features Ltd 12; Rijksmuseum Foundation 28a, 28b; Spectrum Colour Library 13a, 19, 20, 45; Rijksmuseum Vincent van Gogh 26a, 26b; Wyn Voysey 1, 61b; Zefa Pictures 6, 8, 50, 51. The remaining photographs were taken by Ken Patterson and are in the Automobile Association's own Picture Library.

Cover photographs
Main picture and inset (a) Ken Patterson; inset (b) Image Bank

COPY EDITOR *Antonia Hebbert*   VERIFIER *Alison Raines*   INDEXER *Marie Lorimer*

Titles in the CityPack series
- Amsterdam • Atlanta • Bangkok • Barcelona • Berlin • Boston •
- Brussels & Bruges • Chicago • Florence • Hong Kong • Istanbul • Lisbon •
- London • Los Angeles • Madrid • Miami • Montréal • Moscow • Munich •
- New York • Paris • Prague • Rome • San Francisco • Singapore • Sydney •
- Tokyo • Toronto • Venice • Vienna • Washington, D.C. •